DARKNESS AND

LIGHT

DARKNESS AND
LIGHT
MY STORY

JOE THOMPSON
WITH ALEC FENN

First published by Pitch Publishing, 2018

Pitch Publishing
A2 Yeoman Gate
Yeoman Way
Worthing
Sussex
BN13 3QZ
www.pitchpublishing.co.uk
info@pitchpublishing.co.uk

A CIP catalogue record is available for this book
from the British Library.

ISBN 978-1-78531-451-3

Typesetting and origination by Pitch Publishing
Printed and bound in the UK by TJ International Ltd

Contents

Chapter 1

The patient

YOU always remember where you were when darkness clouds your world. It was a Friday night and I was propped up in bed scrolling through Twitter on my phone when the news broke. 'Footballer diagnosed with cancer.' I grabbed the TV remote and turned on Sky Sports, where the same message snaked its way across the yellow breaking news strap along the bottom of the screen.

Shit. My heart sank and my chest tightened. I turned the TV off, tossed the remote on the bed and sat in silence, alone with my thoughts. This time it wasn't my life that was in danger, but the pain still cut deep. I should have been ecstatic – it was only four days since I'd found out I'd beaten cancer for the second time at the age of 28 – but instead I was filled with sadness. I needed to see him and knew he'd want to see me, too.

Three weeks later, I returned to Manchester's Christie Hospital, the scene of my two battles with cancer. The sights and smells were the same: the walls were bleach white, a blur of nurses walked up and down the wards tending to the sick, and the odour of antiseptic handwash filled my nostrils, sparking a thousand memories in my head. For once, I wasn't the patient; I was on the other side of the fence. I was a visitor who was there to try and help.

Wolves goalkeeper Carl Ikeme was rushed to hospital to begin emergency chemotherapy in July 2017 after a batch of routine blood tests during pre-season training revealed he was suffering from acute leukaemia. At 31, football may have saved his life, just as it did mine when I was diagnosed with cancer for the first time aged 24, after falling ill during two games in 2013.

We're both footballers, separated by just three years in age, but I wasn't there to talk about formations or dressing-room gossip. My outfit was tactical and so was my message. I wore my club tracksuit after undergoing a light 45-minute rehabilitation session at the hospital, at the start of my long road back to professional football. I wanted him to see with his own eyes that there was hope and that he could be in my shoes in a few months' time.

You wouldn't have guessed he was the one with cancer. Carl is a mountain of a man, 6ft 4in tall, covered in tattoos, and as broad as a barn door. The nurses did well to find a bed big enough to fit him in. Me? I didn't recognise myself in the mirror. I looked like shit. I'm 6ft 1in but weighed just ten stone, the same weight I was at 16. I lost two and a half stone while I underwent chemotherapy, which also stripped me of my hair, eyebrows and occasionally my dignity when hallucinations reduced me to a naked, quivering wreck.

That's what most people struggle to come to terms with – the slow, physical decline, dragging you down like quicksand. As a footballer, your body is your tool and you work with it every single day to try and become the perfect machine. For as long as I can remember, I've exercised five, six, or even seven days a week. I've eaten what I thought were all the right foods, stretched, shivered in ice baths, prioritised my sleep and rarely touched alcohol. I've done everything right. Those are the sacrifices you make to give yourself a chance in the modern game.

If Carl is anything like me, he probably thought he was invincible, too. Young footballers in the prime of their lives don't get life-threatening diseases, it just doesn't happen. Except, it does. Cancer doesn't discriminate. It doesn't just pick on the old and frail; it attacks children, babies, middle-aged mothers and fathers and even super-fit athletes. It has no respect for beauty, intelligence or love. It comes for whomever it wants, whenever it wants.

His mum wasn't visiting until an hour later, so we had time to have a chat between boys. 'How are you?' he asked me with a smile. 'I'm good,' I replied. 'It's me who should be asking you.' We soon realised we were very similar people. We're both from mixed-race families and come from a world where bravado provides a mask for weakness and much of the communication is delivered in the form of banter. Footballers are brilliant actors; when you first walk into a dressing room you are an outsider and your guard is high. You hide your insecurities at all times and, although you're part of a team, it can sometimes feel like it's every man for himself.

It's the same when you have cancer. You put on a show of strength to let everyone think that you're OK, so they don't worry, when inwardly your mind and body are screaming in pain. But when you're lying in a hospital bed on death's doorstep, there is no time for bullshit. You want the permission to show weakness and ask questions and you want the doctors to be brutally honest with you. I was sensitive to Carl's battle, but I promised to give him an uncensored version of my experiences so he was prepared for what was to come.

His family is his world. He has a wife, Saba, and a little girl, just like me, but his missus was also pregnant with their second child. I knew before I arrived, but it still caught me off guard. I didn't feel qualified to talk about that sort of stuff. He was worried the stress of his illness could trigger a premature labour, and even if it didn't, there was no guarantee he'd be well enough to be by his wife's side when she gave birth. He could also miss those first few months of her life when you bond with your baby.

I know this sounds cold, but I told him to be selfish in the months ahead. He's from Birmingham, but I urged him to base himself in Manchester for the duration of his treatment, even though it's an hour and a half away from his home, family and friends. Christie Hospital is a purpose-built facility for cancer patients, kitted out with the best facilities, technology and staff. I felt it would give him the best chance of winning his fight. Those who really cared about him would jump on a train or drive and make the effort to visit.

I'm convinced that having a small army of close-knit family and friends around me gave me the mental boost I needed to beat cancer twice. The disease attacks the body, but it ravages the mind as well and that's the battle that people don't see on the outside. The treatment is draining, but moral support is like a tap, which fills up your mental reserves. The drip, drip, drip of visitors kept me positive during my lowest moments, even on the days when I didn't have the energy to mutter a response. There were times when my wife, Chantelle, my mum, Michelle, and brother, Reuben, kept me company while I drifted in and out of a medicated sleep.

Carl also had the support of the football world on his side, and I know how powerful that can be. It's a funny old business; team-mates, managers and coaches drift in and out of each other's lives when they move clubs, but as soon as something serious happens they rally round. I remember when I was first diagnosed with cancer I received messages from players I hadn't spoken to for years and others that I'd never even met. It's incredible how quickly people can get your phone number.

I had long conversations with former Aston Villa midfielder Stiliyan Petrov about his fight with leukaemia. His condition was different to mine, but he was still able to tell me how he felt at various stages of his treatment. Bryan Robson also got in touch. He beat mouth cancer in 2011, long after his playing days had finished, but his words were still of comfort. I couldn't believe 'Captain Marvel' knew my name, never mind that he was now talking to me like an old pal. Alan Stubbs, who beat testicular cancer twice, also picked up the phone to talk and offered to help me in any way that he could. My hope was that I'd provide the same beacon of hope for Carl.

The longest hours are those after the lights go out and the visitors are back at home tucked up in their beds. When you're alone in your own thoughts, your head can become a pretty disturbing place to be. When I was tossing and turning during the night, I started to overthink everything. I went over and over the briefest conversations I'd had with my doctor and nurses during the day. 'Was their tone of voice different?' 'Why did they look so serious when they came in?' 'Are they telling me the truth?' There are times when you think you're losing your mind.

You have to find every possible way of distracting yourself from thinking negative thoughts. I read books and had marathon sessions watching Netflix to keep myself entertained, and I told Carl to do the same. I found social media was a blessing and a curse. I enjoyed looking over old pictures of happier times on holiday with family and friends, but scrolling through Snapchat and Instagram and seeing those same people having fun and carrying on with their lives was torture to watch. The thought of my closest friends and family forgetting about me if I didn't survive was a scary one, but a very real one, too.

When you realise something is attacking you from the inside, overnight time becomes precious. Footballers are creatures of habit who crave routine. We like knowing exactly what we're doing and when we're doing it. Order provides calm and a sense of purpose. We're lost without it. During my treatment, every few hours nurses came in to take blood tests or change my chemotherapy bags. Everything was structured. But when that timeline was disturbed it knocked me out of sync. If the nurse was due in at 9:00am and the clock ticked to 9:02am, I'd think, 'Why isn't she here?'

After my first diagnosis, I had to wait six weeks before I started chemo. I've had some bad weeks over the past few years, but they were up there with the worst of my life. I felt like a sitting duck being shot at. I wanted to know why nothing was being done when my symptoms were gradually getting worse and I'd just been told this disease could kill me. You have to trust the process and the experts who have dealt with thousands of patients just like you. But try telling that to a guy who has just read 50 articles on Google telling him he could be dead in six months.

The delay at least gave me the chance to prepare for what was ahead. I spent hours on the Internet looking for answers, just like you do when you're suffering from a cough or a cold. I wanted to find out if there was anything in my lifestyle that could've put me at a greater risk of developing cancer. Sadly, the disease is a faceless criminal that leaves behind very few fingerprints. Still, I made the decision that I would become vegan and start a plant-based diet. That meant cutting meat out of my diet for good. Something had made my body vulnerable to cancer, so I thought it was worth it, even though I didn't know if that was the cause.

Carl is a goalkeeper, so preparation is in his DNA. He'd been reading up on leukaemia and had a good grasp of the ins and outs of the disease. He was also considering becoming vegan and wanted to know how, as an athlete, he'd be able to get enough protein in his body and whether it would affect his performance. I explained that my diet now consisted of beans, pulses, legumes and smoothies to make up for the shortfall, and how I felt energised because my body didn't have to digest meat every three or four hours. He's a switched-on guy, and I knew there were other more serious questions that he wanted to ask.

'So, what's chemotherapy like?' he said. He'd only just finished his first round of chemo, a first taste of the poison, so to speak, and hadn't yet felt its full side effects. There was no point beating around the bush. The truth is, it's hell. The worst thing is the cold feeling as it enters your veins via a drip. It's a hard sensation to describe, but I often compare it to thousands of ants crawling around inside of you. Instinctively your body wants to reject this alien invasion, but you have to keep reminding yourself that they are on your side. The violent sickness comes later. During both of my battles, even the slightest change in temperature would prompt me to throw up and send my weight plummeting.

Hallucinations are often another side effect. I had a few of them during my worst nights, when I imagined various creatures were stood at the end of my bed. I can laugh about it now, but at the time it was scary and I needed a nurse to reassure me I was normal and I wasn't losing my mind. Not all cancer patients have to undergo chemo but after careful consideration I felt it was the best course of treatment. If it meant Carl could live the rest of his life free of the disease, then it was more than worth it. Short-term pain can provide long-term gain.

For all my advice, I knew his battle was individual, as it is with every other cancer patient. Leukaemia and Hodgkin

Lymphoma, the cancer I suffered with, are two different forms of the same disease and we both had a unique, preset DNA, which would respond to it differently. Perhaps his mountainous frame would refuse to wilt under chemo and he may not suffer the same side effects that I did. His mindset would also be different. He'd have his own way of breaking down each minute and hour and overcoming the physical and mental hurdles ahead. One thing was for sure, I knew he was going to put up one hell of a fight.

Visiting time was nearly over when Carl's mother, Jackie, walked into the room to see her son. 'Are you … that guy?' she asked. I knew what she was trying to say. I laughed and told her I was. She reminded me of my own mum; I knew both of them would have swapped positions with their sons to spare them pain. A nurse came in to change his chemo bags, so I said my goodbyes and left the room to give them some space. I told him I'd be back again to see him and he knew I was close by if he needed my help. His mum collared me outside and grilled me with questions out of earshot of her boy. I could tell she was frustrated and wanted to know what he was feeling so she could somehow help him to ease his pain.

I took a minute to ask her how she was because I know all too well that family and friends are also victims when loved ones are battling cancer. I saw first hand the stress it placed on Chantelle, visiting me every day and making me vegetarian meals, while running a home and a family business at the same time. I also remember the white hair that appeared on my daughter Lula's head. I'm convinced that was her body's reaction to bottling up the stress of seeing her dad in hospital.

The disease creates a ripple effect, which leaves very few people untouched.

But cancer doesn't always win and setbacks don't have to define you. I guess, in a nutshell, that's why I'm telling you my story. I had a life long before cancer came along, which had already tasted adversity. When I was a child, I watched my mum get beaten at the hands of my dad. She suffered with mental illness, while he began his descent into a dark world of drugs and crime. At the age of five, I was there when my younger brother, Reuben, was mowed down and dragged under the wheels of a car by a hit and run driver. We were still in primary school when mum was taken away to a mental hospital and our auntie took us to Manchester to start a new life up north.

It wasn't an easy childhood, but it steeled me for what lay ahead. I won the lottery the day I signed for Manchester United. It transformed me from the new kid at school to the king of the playground and provided me with the best sporting education in the world. When they released me just weeks before my GCSE exams, it broke my heart, but not my spirit. I vowed to prove them wrong and to make a career in the game. I hit the reset button and went back down the divisions to achieve my dreams. Impressive? My wife didn't think so when we met for the first time; she wasn't interested in being just another girl dating some 'dickhead' footballer.

Luckily, I convinced her that I wasn't that guy and together we created our own team, along with our daughter, Lula. My two girls were pillars of strength, alongside my mum and brother. Hope also came from other sources. During my first battle with cancer, I shared my journey on the same ward as children as young as four years old. The second time, my teammates were Karl, Dave and Jonathan, three ordinary blokes from different walks of life, who stood by me in the trenches. When sleep was impossible, we talked long into the night about our loved ones and our experiences. Sometimes, we just sat there and laughed at how shit our situation was.

That brief laughter reminded me of being in a football dressing room again, and I made a silent promise to beat the odds and make another comeback. After spending 18 days in an isolation room undergoing a stem cell transplant, I emerged faster than any previous patient at Christie Hospital and returned home to embark upon the lonely road back to football. Those six months transforming a cancer-scarred, ten-stone body into a professional athlete were the hardest of my life, but step by step I climbed the mountain until I reached the summit. The view was beautiful but I still wanted more, and fate granted me a fairytale ending to an incredible script. This is my story ...

Chapter 2
Family

THE sound of my mum screaming as my dad threw her on to the sofa was the soundtrack to one of my earliest childhood memories. The battleground was the living room, where their volcanic relationship had erupted yet again in full view of their first-born. I jumped off the sofa and ran upstairs to the safe haven of my bedroom, where I hid under the covers until it stopped, but trouble was round every corner.

My childhood was like a soap opera; a white mum, an immature black dad and two kids, but the setting didn't quite match the storyline. Our home, where I spent the first eight years of my life, was a box of a flat on the third floor of a housing block on a run-down council estate. It had a basic living room and kitchen, along with two adjacent bedrooms, one of which I shared with my younger brother Reuben.

It wasn't the prettiest of estates, but I didn't grow up in inner city London or a poverty-stricken northern town. The flat was at the top of a steep hill, with a pink blossom tree outside, which overlooked the roads and valleys weaving their way into Bath. The city is a slice of urban paradise, decorated with limestone and sandstone buildings. Tourists flock there to visit the iconic Roman baths and the imposing cathedral, which is famous for its eye-catching gothic architecture.

Beauty and freedom persuaded my mum, Michelle, to start her adult life there after she graduated from Staffordshire University with a degree in English literature and philosophy when she was 23. But she didn't live the dream life she'd imagined when she packed her bags and headed for the bright lights of the big city. In the day she worked at a charity shop called Women's Aid and stacked shelves at Marks and Spencer, before washing pots at the Walrus and Carpenter pub at night.

It was during a shift at the charity shop when she first met my dad, Nicholas. At the time, he was painting the walls of the building as part of his community service after being found guilty of handling stolen goods. She should have known there and then that he was bad news, but his good looks and charisma left their mark. It was another year before they met again, at a nightclub in Bath, but still she resisted his efforts to impress. He persisted with regular visits to M&S, often stalking the aisles she was working on without buying anything, until she eventually gave in.

Together they embarked on a volatile relationship. Dad's charm was a smokescreen for his reckless personality. He is the second youngest of seven children, born to Jamaican parents who moved to England at the end of the Second World War. His mum, Vashtee, or Nanny T as I've always known her, showered him with affection after the tragic death of one of his older brothers. That thirst for female attention has never left him, and my mum was well aware of his reputation as a bad boy with an eye for the ladies when their paths first crossed. But she saw a glimmer of good in him and was convinced she could change his ways.

At first, their relationship was electric. They quickly fell in love in a haze of music and chemistry on the many dancefloors in Bath's city centre and moved in together in the front room of a friend's house. But he wasn't the man my mum's parents had imagined would steal the heart of their young girl. He did try a few courses, such as bricklaying, but found burgling houses and carrying out set-up insurance jobs provided a quicker route to getting his hands on cash and satisfying his impulsive personality. His one steady job, as a DJ who played blues music, meant he often spent his Saturday nights away from home, spinning records in Oxford, Cardiff, Newport, Swindon and Bristol.

His sources of income were almost as unstable as his temperament. At 26, and 14 months younger than mum, he was too immature and selfish for the responsibility of fatherhood when she gave birth to Joseph Jerimiah Lasselles Thompson, three weeks prematurely, on Sunday, 5 March 1989 on the Princess Anne Wing at the Royal United Hospital. It was a tough labour, which lasted 13 hours, before I was eventually dragged out via forceps, weighing 6lb 3oz. But it wasn't my dad who was holding my mum's hand and wiping away tears of happiness – it was my mum's sister, auntie Sue, who was also heavily pregnant at the time.

Several miles across town, Nicholas Thompson was sat on the floor of a jail cell. He'd been arrested after police raided the property they were living in the night before I entered the world. Officers had uncovered his latest treasure trove of stolen goods and slung him behind bars for the umpteenth time. He appeared before Bath Magistrates' Court on the Monday morning, charged with handling stolen goods, and was only spared a jail sentence after the judge decided to show leniency in light of him becoming a father. He escaped with bail and a slap on the wrist.

He was a relieved man, but not because he could now spend his time doting on his newborn son and ensuring the woman he supposedly loved recovered from the trauma of her labour. They had been together for three years, but my arrival was the cue for their relationship to spiral out of control. He became jealous of the time and attention mum gave to me and took out his frustration with regular rounds of verbal and physical abuse. Another method he had of escaping his responsibilities was to tell mum he was going to the shops, only to disappear for a few days to spend his money on weed and chasing women.

Mum's parents, who lived miles away up in Rochdale, were furious, as they could do little to help. Aside from his many personal failings, my grandma Audrey's negative opinion of my dad was also racially motivated. She was ashamed of her daughter for fathering a black man's baby and was horrified at the thought of her friends and other family members finding out. She'd spent nine months largely ignoring her pregnancy before eventually coming to terms with the reality of the situation. I try not to judge her behaviour by today's standards because her view was sadly typical of her generation's attitude towards black men in the 1980s.

After 15 months of bringing me up on her own, mum eventually snapped. Enough was enough, and one afternoon she decided to turn the tables on dad and told him she was nipping out for a pint of milk, only to flee to Glastonbury festival with her friend Lesley, where they both worked on a pancake stall. Back in Bath, dad soon realised he'd fallen for his own trick. He took me to social services that day to complain that mum wasn't fit to be in charge of a baby boy. 'Who is the baby's father?' asked the woman on the desk. Dad turned on his heels and returned home to reluctantly change nappies and prepare bottles of milk.

Mum had escaped reality for a short while, but she couldn't avoid her demons forever, and I'm not just talking about my dad. She's a wonderful person, who is an absolute pleasure to be around when she's on form, but on other occasions she can be like a bull in a china shop, whose mood becomes vicious and quite aggressive. She's a very intelligent woman and that is part of her problem. She is extremely aware of every situation and obsesses over the finest details. If she has a conversation with someone, afterwards she'll overthink everything in her head, which drags her mood down.

Growing up, her behaviour was often erratic. I remember on more than one occasion there was no milk in the house, so she told me to pour water on my Weetabix for breakfast. She often struggled to get up in the morning and get me ready for school. In a normal household, a child would be woken up gently, but not in our house. I remember one time when she banged on the paper-thin walls separating our bedrooms at 4am and told me to put on my school uniform. She quickly realised she'd misread her alarm clock and sent me back to bed, under the instruction to stay in my clothes so I didn't have to get changed again in the morning, which afforded her a little longer to sleep.

Mum certainly isn't lazy, but she'd use up so much energy in the day and then spend hours worrying when she should've been sleeping, meaning she'd end up exhausted and unable to function properly.

I can look back and laugh at it now, but in hindsight it was pretty obvious there was something seriously wrong. Mum was suffering from bipolar disorder, a mental illness that was previously known as manic depression. The condition causes periods of depression and elevated mood. On a good day, the sufferer experiences incredible highs and relentless energy, but can then feel lethargic and low at the drop of a hat. It's caused by a chemical imbalance in the brain and can be triggered by an environmental change or a traumatic episode in everyday life.

Mum had plenty of those to contend with and so did I. Dad's descent into a life of crime and hard drugs was rapid. I could only have been six or seven when he woke me up in the middle of the night with a shake. 'Get your clothes on, grab your coat, you're coming with me.' Minutes later we were outside, pacing through the town centre in the dead of night. We'd been walking for about 15 minutes when dad told me to wait while he walked ahead to meet three associates. They stood there talking for a short while before he returned and took me back home.

I never questioned why he'd taken me with him that night until many years later. At the time I had no idea of the sort of people he was mixing with, but given that he's spent the last 20 years in and out of prison there's every chance they were career criminals or drug dealers. I'm convinced he'd found himself in trouble and wanted me to accompany him to reduce the risk of the situation getting out of hand. Surely the mystery men wouldn't attack him if his little boy, and a potential witness, was watching on close by. He's a coward, plain and simple.

I'm still on a journey to try and understand my dad. There are so many unanswered questions I need to get answers to so I can get closure on my childhood. Years ago, I used to feel my opinion wasn't valid because I hadn't experienced the things he had. I wasn't a father or a husband, but now that I am I've been in his shoes. I want to know how he was capable of hitting a woman in front of his own child. His face is absent from pictures of so many pivotal moments in my childhood, but why didn't he want to watch his two little boys grow up?

The decisions he made baffle me and I've spent many nights trying to find some sort of understanding. My little daughter, Lula, is five. If money was no object and I could spend every day playing arts and crafts with her, or dressing up, I would do. The thought of doing those things with her again and watching her laugh was probably my biggest motivation when I was fighting cancer. Perhaps dad felt he was inadequate because he couldn't provide for his family? Or did he simply choose not to be part of our lives?

He's wasted so much of his life and he's behind bars again now. While I was undergoing chemotherapy he called me to ask me how I was. It was a brief conversation, but I told him once I was better I wanted to come and visit him and ask him all the questions which have troubled me since I was a young boy. He joked that he'd be more than happy for me to see him because he wouldn't be going anywhere for some time. He also promised he would be honest and try to explain his side of the story.

Amazingly, mum and dad stuck together long enough to have a second child. The arrival of Reuben, when I was three, caused another storm in the Thompson household, and this time it was me who was the problem. I don't think I've inherited too many of dad's traits, but for a time I was consumed by a jealous streak as mum divided her time between the two of us. I can't remember it too well, but she tells me I hated him from the moment I saw him and told her to take him back to the hospital.

If she was in the kitchen and he was lying on his play mat, I'd smother him in Sudocrem or talcum powder. I once covered the back of the sofa in marker pen and blamed it on him, despite the fact he wasn't old enough to walk never mind hold a pen in one hand. But the worst incident was when mum came into the living room to find him covered in his own shit. It didn't take her long to locate the perpetrator. A health visitor urged mum to try and get me more involved with him, but I was more interested in hiding his toys from him than showing him any sort of affection.

Our relationship changed almost overnight when he was 21 months old. It was a cold February morning and the three of us were walking to Walcott Infants' Primary School, where I was in my second year. We were running late, so I ran ahead of them and down a narrow ginnel, about 100 yards away from the school gates, which was just about wide enough for a car to squeeze through. But I was stopped in my tracks by the screeching sound of brakes and my mum screaming. I spun around and froze as the driver reversed, dragging Reuben underneath his car before speeding away.

His body was propped up by the kerb, but remarkably he was still alive and even managed to yell at us to go in pursuit of the car. He was covered in orange from head to toe. It's an image I can remember vividly. I can only think it was a combination of blood and some liquid from the underside of the car. He also had a tyre mark down his face, but that was the least of his troubles. Mum was in hysterics as she picked him up and held him in her arms. She screamed at me to run to school and find someone who could call an ambulance immediately. I ran as fast as my little legs could carry me before I came across a teacher who called 999 and then took me inside to comfort me.

Once in hospital, the full extent of his injuries became clear. He had fractured his skull, which required 14 stitches, and hip and also broken his nose and leg. Reuben spent the next six weeks in intensive care before eventually making a full recovery. He still sports the scar on his head and celebrates that day every year as his second birthday. When he was 18, he was given a payout for the injuries he sustained as a child, which helped to pay for some of his university tuition fees.

The shock changed the way I treated him forever, and since that day we've been the best of friends, even if we did occasionally clash when our mock wrestling contests got out of hand. His star sign is Aries, which is pretty accurate, because he's a real fighter at heart. If he wants something, you'd better get out of his way because he'll make sure he gets it, no matter what. He has different qualities to me, having always been very academically gifted and talented at maths. After graduating from Leeds University, he moved to the north-east and now lives in Newcastle, where he works as an accountant. I couldn't be more proud of him and nor could my mum; he's a credit to her and the family.

The incident had repaired our relationship, but it pushed mum to breaking point. While Reuben was in hospital, dad was again nowhere to be seen, and tried to justify his absence by claiming that he despised hospitals. It was left to my mum's friends, Jackie, Maggie and Laura, to help out when she needed someone to look after me while she spent weeks splitting her time between home and the hospital. She was also concerned about my reaction to the incident after my teachers called her in to tell her I'd been drawing dark grey pictures of sad events.

She eventually split from my dad 12 months later. By that point he was spending more time with other women than he was with his family. Years later we found out we had several half-siblings from his casual relationships, which revealed the full extent of his cheating. I have a half-sister, Liberty, who is four years younger than Reuben, meaning he must have fathered her while he was still with my mum. There are also two boys, Malachi and Marley, who were born to two different mothers. I believe there is also one other girl, called Phoebe, who I think has ended up in care because both dad and her mum are now in prison.

This is going to sound like a sweeping generalisation, but his behaviour is stereotypical of a lot of men from Jamaican families, especially in the 80s and early 90s. After visiting the country a few years ago, I realised that many of them believe it's normal to see multiple women at the same time and they certainly don't want to be told what to do by the opposite sex. They also abhor responsibility. A lot of them even have nicknames to go with their alter egos. Dad's was 'Biko' though I'm not sure exactly what it meant. I'd never try to justify his behaviour at all, but all of those things tally with his actions and I can only think he thought they were normal, having grown up with Jamaican parents and frequently visited the country.

I try to keep in contact with my half-siblings because I have nothing against them; it's not their fault they were born into this mess. I don't see them as much as I would like because they all live down in Bath, but they know I'm only at the end of the phone if they need to talk. Our fractured family created a thirst inside me to one day have a solid family of my own. I'd love to have another child as soon as possible, though my chemotherapy treatment means that could be more difficult. I also felt that desire to be part of a solid unit at school, which sparked my decision to start playing football a few years later.

For mum, the pain must've been unimaginable and the way he treated her, combined with Reuben's accident, prompted her breakdown one afternoon when I was eight. My memory of the day is crystal clear. Two ladies from the flats directly above and below our own came inside and sat on the sofa with me, while mum was questioned by three or four psychiatrists. They weren't wearing white coats but they may as well have been. They told us she would be taken to a psychiatric hospital where her bipolar disorder would be closely examined. I was scared and frightened of the unknown. Dad wasn't around and mum was being taken away. What would happen to me and Reuben?

There was a very real possibility that both of us would be taken into care, unless someone was willing to look after us on a permanent basis. My mum's older sister, Bernice, who I still call Nicey because I struggled to pronounce her name as a child, came to the rescue, and not for the last time during our childhood. She couldn't bear the thought of a stranger looking after us and hatched a plan for us to start a new life in Manchester. We would move up north and live with her and her two daughters, which would give mum the time she needed to recover before finding a new place for us to live. Mum agreed. After everything she'd been through she was ready to break free and give her kids the best chance of having a decent upbringing.

I didn't know it at the time, but the first eight years of my life had provided me with some valuable lessons. Bath is a picture of perfection, but you never know what is going on behind someone's front door when the curtains are closed. In every prosperous city there are rats, sewers and poverty. Lots of people head to the city when they're young and go in search of their dreams, but before they know it life has swallowed them up and they're left chasing what might've been. We were lucky, we were still young with our whole lives in front of us. The struggle would eventually be worth it because in the space of a few short months my life would change forever.

Chapter 3

Welcome to Manchester

'WHAT are you looking at you Paki?' Geography clearly wasn't my classmate James's strongest subject and I let him know of his mistake with my fists. We brawled in the school playground in front of a crowd of baying kids before a teacher ran over and brought a premature end to the contest. It wasn't quite the welcome I'd imagined. I'd been at St Vincent's Primary School for about three days, but my classmates still greeted me with suspicion. I didn't look like them and I didn't sound like them either. There were only two other mixed-race children in the whole school, and they weren't keen on another two brown boys joining their flock.

A few weeks earlier my heart was beating with excitement as I stepped off the train and into a new world. Manchester felt so much bigger and busier than Bath, as people hurried past clutching their bags and briefcases and headed off on their journeys. I'd visited a few times before during the school holidays but now it was my new home. Nicey had travelled down to Bath to collect me and Reuben and a few of our belongings and taken us back up north on the train. My uncle Peter was waiting for us through the crowds, ready to lead us on our new adventure. We put our bags into the car and then stared wide-eyed out of the windows as we rolled away from the station and the hustle and bustle of the city slowly disappeared into the distance.

It was early May 1997, I was eight years old, and my destination was Rochdale, a small working-class town on the outskirts of the city. With its terraced houses, high-rise flats and streets lined with takeaways, it didn't have Bath's good looks, but it made up for it with a rugged charm, and it wasn't long before I felt right at home. Nicey lived in a small flat above the family paper shop with her two daughters, Lisa and Michelle. They probably weren't happy that their two little cousins were moving in with them, but they never complained. We squeezed into the three bedrooms, pulled up a couple of extra dining chairs around the kitchen table and made the best of our new surroundings.

The property was on a small estate, which was a little rough around the edges, but it felt sheltered, which we needed after the turmoil of the previous few years. We had a back garden for the first time and lived near a large park, which gave us the freedom to run around and burn off our pent-up energy. It was home for about four months until mum recovered and found a little two-bed terrace for us to live in on a council estate. It was about ten minutes away from Nicey's paper shop, which was an old-fashioned newsagents and a cherished part of the family. My grandma and granddad had owned it before Nicey and uncle Peter had taken it over. It seemed to stock anything and everything, but most importantly it had a penny mix-up tray. Me and Reuben felt like we were in Willy Wonka's factory and would often do chores to ensure that we got a few sweets as a reward for our good deeds.

My auntie is the complete opposite of my mum. She's a sensible soul who goes quietly about her work and likes a simple, peaceful life. Whenever the shit has hit the fan in the Thompson household, which it has done plenty of times over the years, she's the one who has been there to help and if I've ever got a problem I know I can turn to her for advice or shelter, which I needed on many occasions after being thrown out by my mum quite regularly in my late teens over various disagreements and my sarcastic tongue.

Nicey was a teacher at St Vincent's and carried an air of authority, which meant I did as I was told at all times. Within a few weeks of arriving in Rochdale, she had managed to get us a place at the school and made sure the teachers kept her up to date with our progress and an eye on our behaviour. She needn't have worried, there wasn't a chance I'd have crossed her, but unfortunately I couldn't stop other people from crossing me. The playground was a jungle with its own set of rules, which I struggled to navigate in my early weeks. 'Nigger', 'coon' and 'Paki' were three of the welcoming messages I received from the ringleaders of the concrete tribe, who objected to me joining in. I didn't get it.

I pleaded my innocence to the teachers and had to ask my auntie to explain what two of the words actually meant. The boys probably didn't even understand what they were saying, but it opened my eyes to the dangers of ignorance. My daughter Lula is mixed race and I make sure she knows that all humans are born equal, so she doesn't look at other people and think they're different because of their skin colour, hair or body shape. Children are born innocent and it's only when they are exposed to racism and ignorance that they pick up on certain terminology. I think it's one of the biggest challenges as a parent, giving a child freedom but also trying to protect them.

I was thirsty for acceptance and through sport I was granted it. It was obvious to my auntie that I needed an outlet to release my frustrations, so she started taking me to the local athletics club, Rochdale Harriers. Physically, I was one of the smallest children in my group but I soon found out that I had a talent for middle- and long-distance running. I trained in the evenings during the week, and at the weekend I ran the 600m and 800m races, as well as cross country. I would often leave the other lads my age trailing 50 or 100 metres behind me and soon had a reputation around Greater Manchester as the boy to beat.

Athletics gave me the perfect physical education. In football, if you have a blend of speed and endurance, you have got a massive head start over everyone else. Psychologically, I learnt to shorten my races into chunks so it became more manageable in my head, and it's the same when you're playing a game over 90 minutes. If you can chop it up into smaller periods, you can stay focused and stick to a gameplan. I also had another way of mentally zoning out when my legs and lungs were burning as I attacked the hills during cross country and road races. In my head I imagined I was Rocky Balboa running up steps with the theme tune in my head. It was a film my mum had made me watch countless times.

Winning races gave me an identity and also a boost in confidence. My classmates would look at me and say, 'He's the one who does athletics, he's rapid.' It's fickle, but the biggest and fastest boys at school are the popular kids and I quickly went from an outsider to someone people wanted to hang out with, and I still hadn't shown them what I could do with a football. When I arrived in Rochdale I was taken aback by how obsessed people were with football and their local club. It was a tribal mentality I hadn't experienced before, because there are so many teams in Lancashire and Greater Manchester compared to Somerset. I'd only flirted with football on the park with my friend Quinton back in Bath but that began to change. Slowly but surely, I started to make friends, but inside I still felt there was something missing. Athletics was a very lonely sport and I was only enjoying it was because I was winning. In the car on the way to races I'd struggle badly with nerves. Sometimes I'd be sick because of the pressure I was putting on myself and then almost wee myself on the start line. I felt a longing to be part of something; I wanted to be part of a team.

Our two up, two down was only five minutes away from Rochdale Football Club, but at eight years old I'd barely kicked a football and hadn't even been to watch a match. My lack of knowledge didn't put me off and I accepted an invitation to train with the local junior team, in nearby Norden, managed by the dad of one of my classmates. It was within walking distance from home, so my mum didn't need to worry about picking me up and dropping me off. Money was still tight but she managed to save up enough to buy me some boots. It was a big moment for me and I charged up the road one evening for my first taste of grass-roots football. My team-mates couldn't believe how fast I was, but I quickly encountered a big problem. I didn't have a clue about the rules or football tactics, so I was offside all the time. Slowly, my football brain started to develop and before long I'd mastered a simple move: my team-mates would hit the ball over the top and I'd use my pace to run in behind and slot the ball into the net.

At school, my PE teachers noticed that I had a raw talent and took me under their wing. Mr Pegg was a mild-mannered man who suffered with diabetes, which meant he could no longer play football. He loved working with young children and watching them improve. He was the man who gave me a basic understanding of the game. I instantly respected him and felt that the feeling was mutual. He formed a two-man coaching team with Mr Callaghan, who was more of a disciplinarian with a loud voice. With dad out of the picture, they were the first positive male role models I'd had in my life. When you're a small child you want your mum, but once you're in school and start playing sport, you crave your dad's validation. I didn't have one in my life, so Mr Pegg and Mr Callaghan became the men I wanted to impress.

I'd started football later than a lot of the other lads, but within a few months I was banging in the goals for my local club. I was the best player in my school and often played one or two years up despite my slight build. I loved being part of a team. A pat on the back from my team-mates made me feel 10ft tall.

During my career, the times when I've struggled have been when I've felt like an outsider and not a key part of the team. Mentally, I can have doubts when I go out on a pitch, so I need encouragement more than you'd imagine. If you don't know me well, you might think I'm a bit arrogant, but it's just bravado and a front to give an impression of confidence. Football is all about hiding your weaknesses and exposing the opposition's. There's definitely a vulnerability to me as a player and the managers who have understood that are the ones that have got the best out of me.

I'd been playing for less than a year when my team entered a five-a-side tournament in Moston, which pitted some of the best sides in the local area against one another. It was the ideal place for scouts to cast their eyes over hundreds of kids in one afternoon. I remember scoring goals for fun that day, and at the end of it a man called John Cutt approached my mum and coach, Billy Sweetman, and told them he was a scout for Manchester United. He'd been impressed with what he'd seen in the tournament and previous games he'd attended and wanted me to go there for a trial. I didn't know it at the time, but mum was initially reluctant to let me because she knew the chances of me making it were slim and feared my education would suffer. Luckily, she had a change of heart and realised the structure and discipline of academy football could be good for me if I was successful.

United gave me a six-week trial but saw enough potential to offer me a two-year deal after just three weeks. I felt like I'd been handed one of Willy Wonka's golden tickets. Mum didn't drive, so Nicey or a family friend called Jim took me to training on Tuesday and Thursday evenings, as well as my game on a Saturday or a Sunday. It was an incredible time, with the club on the brink of winning the treble. The Class of 92 were in the first team and every young player felt there was a real chance of following in their footsteps. United were also in the process of big changes off the pitch. They were about to sign a multi-million-pound sponsorship deal with Nike, which meant we were kitted out in all the best gear. My first sessions were at the Cliff in Salford before we moved to a brand spanking new base at Carrington. The car park was like football's equivalent of Hollywood's Walk of Fame. On the tarmac, the initials of each player were painted in white. I remember spotting DY for Dwight Yorke, AC for Andy Cole and DB for David Beckham. It was surreal that I was training at the same facility as some of the game's biggest names.

I was given tickets to most home games at Old Trafford, where I realised the type of player I wanted to become. I loved watching Cole and Yorke playing with a smile on their faces. Professional football is a high-pressure environment, but they always looked like they were having a kickabout in the playground. Every weekend they would bamboozle defences with their trademark one-twos and then celebrate in front of the Stretford End. I always try to remind myself that football is fun because once you become a pro and you're fighting for your place and livelihood every week, it's easy to think of it as just another job. I quickly fell in love with United, but secretly I was an Arsenal fan because of Thierry Henry and Ian Wright. They were my idols. I loved that they had an air of arrogance and would exchange verbals with the defenders. They both played with real personality, and as a fan of the game I love players who break the mould and go against the grain.

Surprisingly, I didn't feel pressure when I signed. That might have been because I was so young or maybe I just didn't completely understand the size of the opportunity I'd been given. Academies are often criticised for sheltering players from reality, but it was one of the best experiences of my life. I worked with brilliant coaches like Paul McGuinness, Tony Whelan, Mark Dempsey and Tommy Martin, who all epitomised what Manchester United were about. There was a real emphasis on learning over results. If we lost a game, it wasn't the end of the world. They would explain what we'd done wrong or ask us what we felt had happened and then we'd improve. Every couple of months, I had a one-on-one assessment with them. They gave me ratings out of ten for various areas of my game; for example, shooting, dribbling or passing, and then designed various drills, which would target a particular weakness.

United were also keen for us to have a cultural education by exposing us to different football environments. I played tournaments in America, Spain, France and Holland, where we became used to the pressure of playing knockout football and also some of the perks of being a footballer. When we were in Spain, a group of local kids were desperate for our autographs and waited for hours outside our hotel because they thought we could turn out to be stars in the future. We felt like we'd already made it and happily signed their shirts. I was also surrounded by a talented group of boys, who pushed me to become the best I could be. The likes of Tom Cleverley, Danny Drinkwater, Tom Heaton, Danny Welbeck and Danny Simpson, who have all gone on to have successful careers in the Premier League, were in my age group or around it. It's no coincidence they've gone on to have good careers or why so many footballers have either been on trial or spent part of their youth career at United.

It's fascinating when I look back because those household names weren't necessarily the best in their age groups. The two outstanding players in my team were Sam Hewson and Febian Brandy. Sam was a Frank Lampard-type player who could run box-to-box for 90 minutes and score goals from midfield. But Febian was the star of the side. He had blistering pace and a bag of tricks to beat players. There were times when we'd just give him the ball and he'd win us games on his own. We played Barcelona in a competition in Tenerife and he was named the tournament's best player. Barca were keen to sign him but there was no chance of United letting him go. It's incredible that neither of them went on to have a career at the top level. Febian, who I still keep in contact with, was last playing in Thailand and Sam is at a club in Iceland. It just goes to show that players develop at different rates and ages.

We didn't just learn by playing, we also improved through observation. From time to time, the coaches would allow us to watch the first team train, so we could see at first hand the level we needed to reach if we were going to make it. What struck me was the focus of the players and the manager, Sir Alex Ferguson. They meant business and the pace was relentless. On one occasion, I stood open-mouthed as I watched Ryan Giggs and Paul Scholes take it in turns to practise their shooting. Both of them had won the Champions League and numerous Premier League titles, but they were being given pointers on how to generate more power by lifting both feet off the floor after striking the ball. Scholes's finishing was like a highlights reel of his greatest goals. Every strike, with both feet, seemed to pick out the top corner with ferocious power.

The attention to detail of the manager was frightening. We were playing at a tournament in Shelbourne, Ireland, which Sir Alex attended so he could take a look at the club's next batch of prospects. I can't believe I did it now, but I tapped him on his shoulder and then darted around the other side so he couldn't tell it was me. I was trying to amuse my team-mates, but this wasn't a random bloke in the street, it was the most successful manager in English football. He had eyes in the back of his head and laughed once he caught me: 'I'll remember that,' he said. A few weeks later, I was walking down a corridor at Carrington when he saw me. 'You! Come here,' he said in his Glaswegian accent. 'Was it you who tapped me on the shoulder?' I gulped and looked up at him. I couldn't believe that he'd remembered who I was. 'I hope you're as confident on the pitch as you are with your mates,' he continued. 'Now go on, get yourself to training.' Without hesitation or taking a second look back, I sprinted down the corridor like a child who'd just been given a telling-off by the headmaster.

The importance of maintaining high standards was drilled into us at all times. Turning up five minutes before training or being a couple of minutes late wasn't acceptable. The message was clear; winners make sure they're properly prepared before they go out on to the pitch. One of Roy Keane's favourite quotes, which I read in his book, is, 'Fail to prepare, prepare to fail,' and it summed up the mentality of the club perfectly. I hate being late and will always make sure I'm early for training or social events, and one of the big reasons I'm so punctual is because of the education I had at United. All the academy players were also told to wear black Nike Tiempo boots, so our football made us stand out rather than the colour of our footwear. When we went out on to the pitch we looked military smart. We were all convinced that we were the best players in the country. We didn't play the likes of Arsenal and Chelsea that much, but because of the success of the first team and the quality of the set-up there was a belief that nobody else was doing it quite like us.

At school I was no longer just Joe Thompson. I was Joe Thompson who played for Manchester United. At the back of the class, I'd practise my signature in my books, and daydream of one day doing it for real. My teachers weren't happy and reminded me that, if I didn't make it, I still needed an education to fall back on. I still worked hard at school, but in my head I was convinced I was going to be a footballer. I'd go shopping at the Trafford Centre, but I wouldn't take my tracksuit off because I wanted people to know I played for United. I was proud to represent such a successful club steeped in history and tradition. When you enter your teenage years, temptations start to arise. I had mates who would go to the park for a few sneaky cans of booze or the golf course to mess about, but I was never tempted. Very early on, I understood that I had to live a different life to them if I was going to make it. They would often knock on my door but I'd always say no and tell them I had training the following day.

I loved having a routine and structure to my life. I had a purpose. It was easy for me to go to bed early because I could see the value of being fresh for a match the following day. In the back of my head I had a vision and a goal and was happy to make sacrifices. You speak to so many people who say, 'I could've made it, but it didn't work out.' I didn't want to look back in 20 years and have regrets, that would've killed me. It probably sounds intense given that I was still so young, but the great thing was that there was no pressure on me. Mum never had to force me to go to bed early or be more disciplined. For me, it was always fun and she was happy to join in. She bought herself a pair of Umbro football boots and most nights the three of us would head down to the fields with a pair of pliers, loosen the hinge off the fence, and sneak in to play until it was dark. Not for the first time during my childhood, mum had to play dad, but she never once complained and was liberated by his absence.

I had such an active childhood and I'm using the same approach with Lula. I want her to try as many activities or hobbies as possible and find out what she loves doing. If she follows that, I know she'll be happy. I don't want her to ever feel that she's been forced to go down a particular path. If I have a son in the future, he won't feel any pressure from me to become a footballer. I loved being part of an academy, but I get why some players who have been in one since they were six or seven are sick of football by the time they reach 15 or 16, because there is a lot of external expectation. Normal children just have to worry about their GCSEs, but a teenage footballer has to balance that with a potential sporting career. If their parents are also applying the heat then that can be very difficult to handle at a young age.

For the first time, my life was sailing in calm waters. Our family was happy and settled in Rochdale, and I was content at school and living the dream at United. But there was a problem brewing on the horizon and there was nothing I could do about it. I'd always been a small lad, but as I approached my 16th birthday I was still tiny and really slim. At school, there were boys two or three years younger who were bigger. I felt like most of my team-mates and opponents were towering over me. Football isn't all about being big and strong, but if you're getting thrown off the ball for 90 minutes you've got a problem.

The club were concerned. They told me I looked great in training but had stopped being the same player in games. The truth was that my confidence was shot as soon as I saw I'd be playing against a team of giants. I didn't know how I could affect the game when there was such a difference in size. I felt like I was drowning on the pitch. I had a hand scan at Carrington, which is used to predict a player's potential height once fully developed. The results told me I'd only grow to 5ft 9in or 5ft 10in at a push. It was bad news, and more was to follow.

Chapter 4

The rat race

I REMEMBER the moment I found out like it was yesterday. It was a cold February afternoon and I'd been playing football at the school field with Reuben. We ran home, where mum stopped us in our tracks and ordered us to strip off before setting foot in the house. As always, dinner was nearly ready, but she wanted a word with me first.

I could tell by the tone of her voice that something wasn't right. I walked into the living room, where mum and auntie Nicey beckoned me to join them on the sofa and gave me a reassuring smile. Mum explained that United had called her. The club had decided they weren't going to offer me a YTS contract and would release me in a matter of days.

I sat there dazed and confused, while she tried to soften the blow by saying it would only be temporary and that I'd go to another north-west club, like Bolton Wanderers or Blackburn Rovers, and return to United in the future. I was 15, but I wasn't daft, I knew the truth.

This was the end of the road. I was heartbroken.

A few days later I had a formal meeting at Carrington with two of my coaches, Paul McGuinness and Tony Whelan. They were concerned I was too small and hadn't been affecting games. After the results of my hand scan, they feared I would never be big enough to compete at the top level and felt I'd be better off pursuing a career elsewhere.

It felt like my world had stopped rotating on its axis. I tried to be brave and thanked them both for everything they had done for me over the previous seven years, but inwardly I was devastated. On the journey home I didn't say a word, and when we got back I retreated to my bedroom to lick my wounds.

In the days that followed I barely moved. My friends knocked on my front door to see if I wanted to join them for a game, but I didn't answer and kept the news to myself. My overwhelming emotion was rejection. I felt like I'd been kicked in the stomach. My self-esteem was intertwined with my football ability, so now I felt worthless.

When you play for United, you're used to everyone telling you you're amazing and that you're going to make it. That makes it even more difficult to take when the rug is pulled from under your feet. At school, I used to feel like the corridors parted when I walked down them – everyone wanted to be Joe Thompson. But when United let me go, I felt like people were pointing and laughing at me. Some of them probably were. Some kids relished the fact they could have a sly dig.

When I finally told my closest mates I'd been released, they supported me, but other people would come up to me and say, 'Are you not at United now?' even though they knew full well that was the case. I realised very quickly who my allies were. Some so-called friends weren't interested in socialising with me anymore because my star was no longer shining quite so brightly. From that moment on, I vowed to keep a tight circle and became wary of letting other people in.

The news couldn't have come at a worse time. It was only a few days before my 16th birthday and my GCSE exams were in a few months' time. My teachers had warned me for years that I needed to knuckle down and make sure I got good enough grades to pursue another career, while I practised my signature on the back of my books. Their words had come back to haunt me and it hurt. I felt like a few of them wanted to come up to me and say, 'we told you so'.

At that age, your hormones are up and down like a yo-yo and it's difficult to process setbacks. I struggled to sleep at night and my mum would often put lavender oil on my pillow to help me switch off. Motivation was also in short supply. Until that point, I was more concerned with what my coaches had to say about my passing or finishing when we had our regular assessments than anything my teachers had to say. I wasn't stupid, though. I knew if I didn't put the work in, I could end up with no club and no qualifications. Talk about a fall from grace. I had to fix up and do it fast.

I decided to go back to basics and start playing for my school team. Since the day I signed for United, I hadn't been allowed to play for any other team, to make sure I didn't suffer an injury. I was back with the boys and in a way it felt liberating. The pitches were bobbly and before the games we had to put the nets up and bring them down again afterwards, which I'd never done before. It was football in its purest form and there was less pressure. Even though we were all desperate to win every game, I didn't have to worry about facing giants who would dominate me physically. Having been at United, I became a target for lads from other schools, and some of their tackles weren't far off GBH. But part of me liked that. As a winger, if defenders are smashing you, it means you're doing something right.

The standard felt easy compared to United. Time and time again, I'd stand on the touchline wide on the right wing, breeze past three or four players and cut the ball back for one of my team-mates to score. Slowly, that success helped to rebuild my self-belief. We managed to reach the cup final and I scored one and assisted another in a 3-1 win. It was just the lift I needed and the perfect way to end our school days together. Football felt like fun again. Although I loved my time at United, as you get older you realise you're playing for a contract or to impress your coaches before your next assessment. The scrutiny is intense and you know that if you put a foot wrong there is someone else, just as good as you, who is ready to take your place. You have to have a professional mindset from a very young age, and although I was comfortable with that it can strip away the fun.

I wasn't ready to throw in the towel. At every club, you meet players who have been released at least once but have possessed the character to bounce back and forge a career in the game. Some lads never recover from the trauma of that first setback. Others realise they just don't want it enough or simply don't have the talent to cut it at a professional level. Some boys discover alcohol and girls, especially around 16.

I knew I hadn't become a bad player overnight and I had a head start in the rat race to find a new club. Hundreds of other lads would find themselves in the same situation as me over the coming months, but being released in February meant I had the chance to make an early impression.

Liverpool were interested, but mum knew the competition would be tough and thought it would be better for me to be a big fish in a smaller pond. My first trial was at Blackburn, who were a decent outfit and their academy had a good reputation. I felt I did well, but they weren't taking players on until the end of the summer and told me they would be in touch then. I was confident they would make me an offer, but I couldn't put all my eggs in one basket. Wigan were in League One, so I went along to train with their youth team. The training ground was surprisingly good, not quite up there with Carrington, but still a quality facility. They had a couple of players who had been at United and they had told me good things about the set-up, while I'd also played them on multiple occasions, so I knew they had a decent side.

I did well but didn't get on with one of the coaches. I didn't like his delivery of criticism and the way he went about his sessions. I probably had a bit of a chip on my shoulder as well, which didn't help. I came home and told mum I didn't want to go back, but she urged me to give it a bit longer. Reluctantly, I agreed, and the club told me they liked me. I was playing with the under-17s and 18s and holding my own. That gave me confidence, because I was playing with older, bigger lads, and doing well, despite my skinny frame. But just as I'd started to come around to the idea of joining them, I turned up to a training session to find out it had been cancelled. Nobody had even bothered to tell me or my mum. It was unprofessional and would never have happened at United. That was the end of my time at Wigan.

As summer approached, I was still without a club, until my teacher, Mr Eyres, threw me a lifeline. He knew a coach at Rochdale and said they were interested in taking a closer look at me. I had nothing to lose, so once my exams were finished I went along to training one night. Their facilities were an eye-opener. There was no training ground as such; instead they played on an old school, sandy astroturf pitch in Heywood, which had hockey nets on it. I thought to myself, 'Jesus, what am I doing here?' I had to take along my trainers and mouldies and inspect the pitch before deciding on my footwear. I went for trainers to be on the safe side. The training session didn't feel structured and the players didn't even wear training kits. I had been spoilt rotten at United – everything was Nike and brand new – but I had nowhere else to turn.

That night was also the first time I met Keith Hill. He was in charge of the youth team at the time and came along to cast his eye over potential recruits. He had been an old-fashioned brute of a centre-back during his playing days and must've only just retired, because he still looked like a footballer. He had a big set of quads on him and rolled his shorts high and his football boots were always black. He liked what he had seen and invited me to play for the youth team that weekend. We were playing against Halifax at Rossendale United's ground, just outside Burnley, which felt like a million miles away from Carrington. I was playing against third year pros, who were 19, but I got my chance off the bench in the second half. I did well and managed to score a goal late on when I nicked the ball off the centre-back and slotted home past an onrushing keeper.

We won 2-1 and I felt I had the backing of the dressing room, but after the game I was reminded of my innocence. All the lads stripped off and headed to the communal showers with their cocks out. I was shocked. I was only 16 and didn't have the same confidence as the older boys. I got in the showers with my boxer shorts on, which prompted laughter from a few of them. 'Don't be shy mate, get it out, we've all got one!' said a lad called Deano. I did as I was told. It was a character-building experience to say the least. I was out of my comfort zone and learning fast about the inner workings of football dressing rooms. I may have impressed my team-mates with my performance on the pitch, but I still had to do a lot more to get Keith's seal of approval.

'Take those fucking earrings out and give them back to your grandma,' he bellowed in his thick Bolton accent, to the amusement of the lads. It was the week after the game, but I immediately realised I'd only passed stage one of his test. I've never been shy to dress a bit differently and had decided to get both my ears pierced. I thought they looked the part, but he wasn't a fan of my cubic zirconia diamonds. It was a stupid mistake, particularly when I was trying to make a good impression. He probably thought I was trying to be different, but I had completely forgotten to take them out. Still, I couldn't believe he was hammering me after I'd scored the winner at the weekend. I realised there and then that he wasn't the sort of manager to put an arm around your shoulder. He preferred a tough love approach. He was testing me to see how I would react. Would I go into my shell or try to prove him wrong?

I went home that night and moaned to my mum. 'This guy is like a drill sergeant, all he does is shout and swear.' I was unsure of Keith at first, because he was a real man's man and very intimidating, whereas I was still a boy. He is black and white and says it how he sees it, but I grew to appreciate his honesty. There is no bullshit with him. He has actually calmed down a lot now. Don't get me wrong, you still fear a bollocking from him, but he has definitely mellowed and understands that different approaches work with different players. Luckily, we got on well after earring-gate and he was incredibly supportive during both my battles with cancer and never once pressured me to return quicker than I needed to. I'll always respect him for that.

Keith kept asking me to train with the youth team, so I must have been doing something right. A few weeks later, he named me in his side to play against Bolton. The youth-team ground was at Bowlee fields in Heywood, a small town just outside Rochdale. The changing rooms were dark and primitive and there was an overwhelming smell of Deep Heat. At the time, I didn't even know what it was. I was used to tiger balm and nice massage oils at United, but the Rochdale lads would spray cans of the stuff on their legs, along with dollops of cream, to try and get rid of any muscle soreness before the games. I sat in the corner and watched on as the lads went through their pre-match routines. I was fascinated by their little idiosyncrasies. Some of them would roll their socks up to a specific height, while others wrapped tape around them to keep their shinpads in place. I'd never seen so many pairs of Copa Mundials in my life, with big long studs so they would keep their footing on muddy pitches.

Bolton were in the Premier League at the time, so it was no disgrace that we got beat that afternoon. I played well again, and after the game I called my auntie to ask her for a lift back home. She couldn't pick me up and my team-mates had all left, so I had to walk into Heywood to catch a bus. I had no idea where the nearest stop was, so I walked for 20 minutes or so until I came across one. I put my bag down and waited. Up the street, a minibus pulled up and a group of war veterans climbed out. They were all wearing military uniforms, which proudly showed off their medals and various badges. They started walking towards me when one of them shouted, 'you fucking monkey'. I was momentarily stunned and thought I must've imagined it. There were about 30 of them, and as they got closer the same guy started waving his walking stick and yelled, 'You heard, you fucking monkey. Do you think I fought a war to have your types come to my town and sit on your lazy arse?'

My first reaction was laughter. I was incredulous and couldn't believe what I was hearing. They were all heading to a local working men's club for a drink. Worryingly for me, the entrance was just behind the bus stop and I feared they might come out again later on and start looking for trouble. I could've reacted badly, but I decided to let their comments slide. They must have been 70 or 80 and had probably done and seen things I can't even imagine. They were just ignorant and hadn't changed with the times. Thankfully, the bus eventually arrived and I jumped on without taking a second look back. When I got home I told my mum but she just laughed. She didn't condone what they'd said, but I think she'd become used to those sorts of comments from older people, especially when she first started seeing my dad.

They were testing times, but it made me realise how much I wanted to make it. I loved the grittiness of football at that level. In England, we talk a lot about the character you need to play lower down the leagues, but, really, it is nothing compared to what a lot of foreign players have to conquer before they come to Europe. Many South American and eastern European footballers have to contend with sand or concrete pitches until their teenage years. Still, playing lower down the leagues requires a certain steeliness because it is more exposed. Everything is a bit rougher around the edges and there are none of the comforts you enjoy in an academy. It was the best experience I could have had at that age. It was a real eye-opener. I saw at first hand the mentality and professionalism required if I was going to make it and was convinced that I had the tools for the job.

After four months of training with Rochdale, the club at last offered me a two-year YTS contract. I was only 16, but Keith was keen to play me as much as possible, even at the expense of the second- and third-year players. That probably wouldn't have happened elsewhere, so it was the perfect place for me to develop. In your first year, you are assigned specific tasks you have to carry out in the first-team dressing room. A typical day began at 8:30am and ended at 4pm. The first job of the morning was scrubbing boots, which I loved, because the smell of the polish was beautiful. I used to love buffing the boots, trying to get them as shiny as possible. A nod of approval from the first-team players told me I was doing a good job. After that, we'd run a bath and put cones and discs in there, making sure that there was no mud left in between the little grooves in the plastic. If we didn't play well, the jobs became more menial. After one bad defeat, we all had to bring a toothbrush with us to training and scrub the dressing room tiles and get stuck into the grouting, making sure everything was gleaming.

When the clock struck 4pm, I didn't want to go home. I'd happily have stayed there for a few more hours. I loved being around the first-team dressing room; there is nothing else quite like it. You would hear all sorts of stuff about girls and the banter they'd had with their mates, which you just wouldn't get away with talking about in a normal office. Every young player has to do an initiation song, which I think is a brilliant way of integrating new players, but it's a ruthless couple of minutes. The build-up is nerve wracking, and if you're rubbish you get heckled and various items are thrown at you, but it's all good fun. I remember I had to stand on a Lucozade box and belt out my song. I can't remember exactly what I sang, but I think it was something by Shaggy. My voice isn't the best, but I got a round of applause and I think they respected the fact I put my hand up to be one of the first to do it.

We were only young but we were like a pack of hyenas and weren't afraid to challenge the first team. We were always cheeky and would push the boundaries to see how much we could get away with. On the training pitch I would often try to nutmeg the older players and then shout 'megs' on the occasions I managed to slip the ball through their legs. If there was a tackle to be made, we made it properly. We weren't going to be intimidated. That is the way it should be. It is a dog-eat-dog game and eventually we wanted to take their places, so we made sure we competed from day one.

I was a youth-team player but would often train with the first team. The club were in League Two and the style was very different to what I was used to. There was more of an emphasis on getting the ball into the channels and then going from there, rather than playing it out from the back. I had to adapt, but I was surprised by how good the players were technically. Paddy McCourt was a brilliant talent who could waltz through teams at will. Grant Holt and Rickie Lambert also stood out. I remember watching Rickie practise free kicks after training had finished. The consistency of his ball striking was incredible. The goalkeeper had set up a wall with four mannequins and knew exactly where he was going to put it, but he kept picking out the top corner. Once he was done with one side he then started finding the opposite one with ease. Playing with them made me a better player. I could stand the ball up at the back post and Lambert would win it every time. If I found Holt with a pass, the ball would stick to his chest, knee or foot.

Lambert was a wonderful role model to have at that time. He was on Liverpool's books as a kid before they let him go when he was a teenager. Blackpool signed him as an apprentice when he was 16, and he made his debut a year later, but only played a few games in the old Second Division before he was released. He was a free agent for nearly four months and spent time working in a beetroot bottling plant to make ends meet, until Macclesfield Town offered him a contract. Just over a decade later, he was scoring goals in the Premier League with Southampton and playing for England. Despite his obvious talent, if you'd told me he'd become an international when he was at Rochdale, I wouldn't have believed you. It just goes to show what you can achieve if you work hard and refuse to give up.

It's easy to dismiss the ability of players outside the Premier League, but there is a lot of quality lower down the leagues. There are so many players who have been released by top clubs before forging a career in the Football League. There is definitely a big difference, technically and physically, between the elite and the bottom end of the Football League, but the gap is minimal between the Championship and League Two. That's why I think it's so important for young lads to go out on loan to see what level they are at. I maintain that academies are great for nurturing talent, but playing against grown men, who are fighting to win and pay their mortgages every month, is a much sterner test than a development squad game on an empty training ground.

I was growing up fast and beginning to find my own identity. After leaving United, I felt I'd lost part of mine, but I was starting to develop an individual streak now. That started with getting a pair of boots that fitted my personality and playing style. I wasn't on a lot of money, just the standard YTS wage of £55 a week, so I asked my mum if she'd buy me the silver Nike Mercurial Vapor boots, which Thierry Henry and the Brazilian Ronaldo used to wear. At United, we only ever wore black boots, so it was exciting to be able to wear something else. If you wear silver boots and play on the wing you instantly become a target, but I didn't mind that. It puts a bit of pressure on you to deliver. If you wear bright colours and don't have the courage to get on the ball and make things happen then you probably shouldn't be wearing them.

After a dark few months, my confidence had returned and it was boosted further by my GCSE results. I managed to come out with an A*, four As, four Bs and a couple of Cs. I'd done that well, my mum didn't believe me when I ran back to the car and told her. There was another Joseph Thompson in the same year group, who has since gone on to become a doctor, and she asked me if I was sure there hadn't been a mix-up. Thankfully, the results were all mine. I was on a roll and felt like nothing could get in my way.

Chapter 5

Losing the L plates

THERE'S nothing quite like a good training session to put a spring in the step of an apprentice footballer. Well, that and the sight of an attractive female. The sun was shining as I headed home one afternoon, when I was halted in my tracks by a pretty girl across the road. She was tall, with long dark hair, and dressed pristinely from head to toe. I swung my bag over my shoulder and strutted over to her to say hello.

Lucy Marsh was my first girlfriend, but we lived very different lives. I was a 17-year-old apprentice footballer and she was a 16-year-old student at Bury Grammar School. She lived in a beautiful house, in an area called Milnrow, about 15 minutes away from me, on the other side of Rochdale. After our first date at the local cinema, her mum picked her up in a drop-top Mercedes SLK, while I waited for a taxi. Her dad was a well-respected businessman, who made his money from turning around fish and chip shops and selling them on. At weekends, him and his son, Tom, played golf together.

I was inspired by the life Lucy's parents had provided for their children through years of hard work. They were the example of the solid family unit I wanted to build for myself when I was older. At the time, the prospect of driving an expensive car or living in a posh house was a distant dream. My YTS contract, which is for youth-team scholars between the ages of 16 and 18, was just £55 a week. Not that it mattered; getting paid to play football seemed like a pretty good deal when most teenagers my age were working part-time jobs in shops and supermarkets. My modest wage also kept me hungry to win a professional contract and, although I didn't know it at the time, it wouldn't be long before Rochdale tied me down to senior terms.

Steve Parkin and his assistant, Tony Ford, handed me my professional debut at the end of the 2005/06 season. I'd only just turned 17 but was named on the bench for a Tuesday-night game at home to Carlisle United and came on for the final ten minutes. I played on the right wing and came up against a veteran Spanish left-back with long hair called Igor Aranalde. He was vastly experienced, but he had no pace and I fancied my chances of showing him up. Little did I know, his speed was in his head. He did everything with one touch and I couldn't get near him. I'd learnt my first lesson: brain always triumphs over brawn.

We lost 2-0 that afternoon against a quality Carlisle team, which included players like Karl Hawley and Danny Graham, who would go on to have good careers higher up the divisions.

LOSING THE L PLATES

It wasn't the ideal result, but I was buzzing to have made my first appearance and loved playing in front of a real crowd. My tournament experience at Manchester United, where we often played in front of thousands of fans, prepared me for the booing, emotion and pantomime of matches. At one tournament at PSG's Parc des Princes stadium, there were over 10,000 supporters watching our games, so I felt at ease playing in front of a couple of thousand people at Spotland.

I wasn't the only youngster who made his debut that night. Theo Coleman, who I'd played alongside at Manchester United and for Rochdale's youth team, started the game on the left wing. He's one of my best mates and also one of the most naturally gifted footballers I've ever played with. He was blessed with incredibly fast feet and should've gone on to play in the Premier League, but his attitude just wasn't right. United released him because he didn't put the effort in, and he left Blackburn Rovers and Burnley for the same reason before ending up at Rochdale. I'm not exaggerating when I say that he was better than Raheem Sterling at the same age.

His demise reminds me a bit of Ravel Morrison's. Theo needed to play in a team where the other ten players would do his running for him, so he could concentrate on getting on the ball in the final third. I know his unfulfilled promise bothers him now he's a little older and wiser. I still remember Keith's words the day he signed him: 'You'll either leave here for millions or you'll go and work night shifts somewhere, so people won't recognise you.' He wasn't too wide of the mark.

I knuckled down and was handed my full debut away to MK Dons in the first month of the following season. They were one of the best sides in the league, with the likes of Keith Andrews, Lloyd Dyer and Izale McLeod in their side. I was buzzing that the manager trusted me to not only start but also play the full 90 minutes against a quality side. There was no chance of me getting carried away, though, because I had another unofficial role – tea boy on the first-team coach. It wasn't the most glamorous of jobs, but I loved being in that environment.

The coach had its own social structure. The front was reserved for the manager and coaching staff, while the back was where the bad lads and jokers would assemble to play cards. As soon as the journey started, numerous copies of the *Racing Post* would appear and the lads would start picking out their bets for the weekend. After they'd made their selections, they'd read the newspapers and see what journalists and opponents had been saying before the game.

In my early days, I would sit and watch in fascination. I remember on one away trip to Torquay, I was on my feet for about six hours, making teas and coffees. Darrell Clarke, who is now manager of Bristol Rovers, is one of the funniest blokes I've ever met, and he decided to stitch me up. We could clearly see their ground getting closer and closer, but Darrell decided to play dumb. 'We've been travelling for hours, where is the ground?!' he said. 'It's there Clarkey, it's there!' I shouted and pointed out of the window. The whole coach burst out laughing. They'd successfully reeled in another victim.

I always got on with the older players and loved hearing the stories they had to tell, but I was petrified of a scouser called John Doolan. He's a coach at Everton now and we still talk every now and then, but when I was 17 the sound of him shouting at me in his thick accent when I gave the ball away or didn't pass to him shook me to my boots. I wasn't scared of facing him on the pitch, but if I saw him walking down the corridor he'd give me a jab and say, 'Good morning, how are you?' The other lads had their own ways of keeping me in check. I was still on boot cleaning duties and if I'd played well in training they'd throw their boots at me to scrub with a little more venom.

Someone else who enjoyed doing that was Keith Hill, who replaced Steve Parkin in February 2007, with the club mired in the relegation zone. He was initially given the job on a temporary basis but guided us to a ninth-place finish to win a permanent deal. It was a remarkable achievement. His bullish style was the same as it was with the youth team, and it got the best out of that group of players. It was an experienced squad, with lads who had children, mortgages and little businesses on the side. They weren't little boys, they were grown men with very real responsibilities and their maturity was a big reason we were able to get out of trouble and escape relegation.

Keith had made the bold move to place his faith in youth and promoted several lads to the first team. His approach with me remained the same. If he saw me getting excited about anything he'd be there like a shot to put me down. I once read a quote from Will Smith that said you need to fan someone's flame to get the best out of them, but Keith has never fanned mine. He's probably the only manager who can compliment you one minute and then retract it almost immediately. He would often say to me, 'You played really well today, but you lost the ball here and should've passed it there. In fact, you only played ok.' Sometimes I would think to myself, 'Do you ever praise me?' He would never change his approach with me, which is fine, because I knew he just wanted to get the best out of me.

Outside of the game, we didn't speak that much. When I was diagnosed with cancer he danced around it and spoke about everything else apart from that. I suppose that was his way of trying to keep my spirits up by avoiding talking about my illness. I've got massive admiration for him and he's taught me a lot about character and the importance of having strong values. It's relentless and tough under him, because he doesn't miss a trick. If you think you can hide or not make a run, he will see it. He gives you the freedom to make decisions but he also demands a lot from you. Once you've played under Keith, you realise it won't ever be tougher under anyone else. His favourite motto is, 'one singer, one song'. Basically, do it his way or find somewhere else to play.

At that point, I didn't have an agent. A few of my older team-mates had pointed me in the direction of some reputable people, but I didn't feel I'd clicked with any of them. That changed when I met Gary Lloyd. He was a small guy with ginger hair and walked round with his chest puffed out at all times, exuding confidence. He reminded me of Ari Gold, the talent agent played by Jeremy Piven in the TV show *The Entourage*. We were the complete opposite in appearance and personality, but we connected from the minute we sat down at a hotel not far from the ground. At the time he had a very small stable of players on his books, including Glenn Murray and Gordon Greer. I preferred quality over quantity and felt if I was with someone with fewer clients I'd get a bit more of his time. He also told me he'd be able to get me free pairs of Nike boots, which I knew would save me a few hundred quid a year.

Lloydy lived in Manchester and seemed to know everyone in the city. He was good friends with Ryan Giggs and went to United games with him when they were kids. His background was in accountancy, so I knew that he knew his stuff from a financial point of view. Players often ask friends to represent them, who don't have any business experience, which is a dangerous avenue to go down. When it came to striking a deal, Gary was like a Jack Russell. I remember being sat in his car once while he was negotiating a new deal for one of his players with the chief executive of a club. He had the phone on loudspeaker and suddenly started hustling and haggling like nobody I'd ever met before. I liked that side of him; he would always do his absolute best for his clients.

We shook hands but never signed a contract. We had a gentlemen's agreement that if either of us ever felt that it was time for us to go our separate ways, we would do so with no hard feelings. Agents get a bad reputation because there are crooks within the game who are desperate to make a fast buck, but having a good one is so important. The last thing you want when you're negotiating a contract is an agent who is so far wide of the mark with his numbers that he antagonises your current club or jeopardises a move elsewhere. In the event I left Rochdale, I needed someone acting on my behalf who knew what they were talking about when it came to transfers. As a player, you just want to concentrate on your football and leave the numbers to an expert.

Lloydy and I agreed that he would receive a fixed percentage of my weekly wage as well as a cut of any other deal he struck for me. For example, if I agreed a new contract and received a signing-on fee, he would get a slice. His financial expertise was useful outside of football as well. When I bought my first house I ran everything by him. He knew how much I was likely to earn over the following couple of years and advised me on the size of mortgage I could afford to take on. He was always very honest with the advice he gave me and I appreciated that. Some agents will tell players to do things that benefit them rather than their clients, but he made sure there was no chance of me frittering away my cash.

My market value was given a boost when I was nominated for the League Two Apprentice of the Year award at the end of the season, which is given to a young player who has excelled on the pitch, but also in their studies. I'd just turned 18 and was in my final year at college, where I was studying for a BTEC sport diploma, which was all about anatomy, physiology and fitness. I attended a local college twice a week, but initially failed my first year after taking my eye off the ball. It wasn't like me, I'd always done well at school, and I had to knuckle down and get a distinction in my second year to ensure I passed the course.

There was a big ceremony at Grosvenor House in London to announce the winner and various other prizes. I travelled down on the train with the gaffer, his new assistant, David Flitcroft, my agent and our chief executive. I had no idea I was going to win it, and I was stunned when my name was read out on stage. The prize served as a rubber stamp, which gave me confirmation that I had the quality to have a real future in the game. When I stood up to receive the trophy, I looked around the room and saw hundreds of other professionals applauding me. 'I want more of this,' I thought to myself. It was a big moment at the start of my career and the trophy still sits proudly on my mantelpiece at home.

I knew that Wigan and Southampton had been watching me, and Rochdale were keen to ward off any potential suitors. They offered me my first professional contract before the end of my YTS deal, worth £150 a week, plus game-related bonuses. It was a lot of money to me back then and meant I could help my mum out by contributing to the running of the house, even if it was only £50 a week, and still have some left over for myself. But I wanted more. At the time, I felt I was probably the best player from my age group in the north-west. I'd been to college with Oldham, Bury and Burnley players, and I knew a couple of them were earning £150 per week. They hadn't made the same progress as me, so I felt I deserved to be paid more.

I dug my heels in, turned down their opening offer and asked for another £50. They must have thought I was a cheeky bastard for trying to barter with them after they'd just offered me the chance of a lifetime. I had nothing to lose – if I couldn't squeeze another £50 a week out of them, I'd immediately sign on the dotted line. That's a part of my character that I like. I'm a nice person, but I know I can dig my heels in and stick to my guns. In the end, they agreed to give me a two-year contract on £200 a week, which was topped up with appearance and goal bonuses. I tried to wangle an assist bonus as well because that was a big part of my game, but they weren't having it. If I made over ten starts, then my wage would rise to £300 a week in my second year.

The carrot had been dangled in front of me and I was determined to grab it. I didn't go on holiday that summer and did a lot of additional fitness work so that I returned for pre-season in the shape of my life. Our strength and conditioning coach gave me a programme to build up my strength and power. I did a lot of Olympic lifts, which are full body exercises requiring you to move weight at speed, so you develop explosive power. I was conscious that my body needed to be strong enough to be able to potentially play two games a week and also compete with fully grown men on a more regular basis.

The close-season is a paranoid time for footballers. As a young professional you find yourself wondering what everyone else is doing. As you get older that changes because you know what is required and you understand it's important to switch off. But for the first two or three years of my career I never really stopped. I'd play five-a-side, go for a run or head to the gym most days so I didn't lose my fitness. I feared that someone else was doing extra and I'd get shown up when I needed to make an impression. When you're a teenager, there are question marks hanging over you because the manager still hasn't seen enough of you to know he can trust you. You have to start building your reputation and show that you're a reliable professional.

Another threat is the arrival of new signings. When they enter the dressing room for the first time, you welcome them but you also size them up, especially if they play in your position. You're also wary of too many new faces rocking the boat and changing the group dynamic. If there are too many signings you can lose the identity of the squad very quickly. I think it's one of the hardest things for a manager to get right. You can identify a talented player, but finding out what he's like as a character and how he'll integrate into the group is more difficult. What's his character like when the chips are down? How does he respond when he gets shouted at? Does he need an arm around him? You want players to come in who will improve the team but also the spirit of the group.

You often see what a player is made of on the first day of pre-season, when you get your body fat measured. If a player has put in the hard yards during the summer, he should be 10 per cent or below. Mine is normally about 7 per cent, but at 18 it was only 5 per cent and there was next to no muscle on me. I was 6ft tall but rake thin. I was physically slight but at least I'd proven the wrist scan I had at United had been completely wrong.

The beep test is another dreaded obstacle. If you haven't heard of it, it involves running continuously between cones, 20 metres apart, and turning before each beep sounds. At each stage, the time between each beep gets progressively shorter. If you can't reach the cone and turn in time you have to drop out and you're then given a score based on the number of shuttle runs you've completed. You need to make a good impression or else you look like you've been slacking. There's an element of fear before you do it, which I've learnt is a good thing, because it shows that you care. There can't be many industries like football where you're subjected to a battery of tests. That's probably another reason why some players don't make it, because they don't deal well with the stress of being judged on a daily basis.

Once pre-season started, I made sure I had very few distractions. I'd see my girlfriend, Lucy, a couple of times a week, but apart from that football was my sole focus. I only lived a stone's throw away from the ground, so I'd walk there for the morning session and then use the gym in the afternoon. After finishing at 3pm, I'd return home, sleep, eat my dinner and then get an early night. It was a relentless schedule for about six weeks, but I loved the routine and the confidence I gained from getting fitter, faster and stronger.

I'd put in the hard yards and was determined to nail down a first-team place, but I didn't kick on as much as I expected. The team was doing really well, so I found myself in and out of the side. There were still highlights, though, including my first goal in a 3-1 win over Darlington at home, though it was very nearly a disaster. During the warm-up my boots split and my spare pair had moulded studs, which I couldn't wear in the wet weather. Ten minutes before kick-off I had no boots to play in. Luckily one of the lads, Simon Ramsden, had a spare pair of size nine Nike Vapors, but they were brand new and were killing my feet. I had a nightmare start to the game and barely touched the ball, but then out of nowhere Tom Kennedy swung a ball into the box and I headed home on the penalty spot, a bit like Patrick Kluivert did in his heyday.

When I was playing well I enjoyed getting involved in a bit of confrontation on the pitch, and I remember celebrating by putting my finger to my lips to the Darlington fans, who had given me stick before my goal. My mum still has that picture of me celebrating at her house. My confidence was high and I set up Glenn Murray to score our second goal. My performance saw me named in the League Two Team of the Week, but I wanted more and wasn't involved as much as I wanted to be. I was still only 18/19, so I knew I couldn't complain too much, and the most important thing was that the club was on the front foot. Keith Hill was moving us forward and I'd developed a really good relationship with our assistant manager, Dave Flitcroft. He was a very funny guy and we bounced off each other. You could have a laugh with him during the week, but on a Saturday afternoon he was serious.

We finished fifth in League Two, which meant we faced Darlington in the play-offs. The team spirit was fantastic, aided by a healthy balance of older pros and young lads. Every Friday, after the final training session of the week, someone would be picked out for giving the ball away more than three times and would have to put some money in the team kitty, which we used for a night out at the end of the season. There was a dispute between Lee Thorpe and Rene Howe over who was the worst offender, so they settled it with an arm wrestle on the team coach on the way to Darlington.

They were both strong lads and it was a stalemate until Thorpey's shoulder popped out of his socket and snapped with an audible crack. The bone just flew out of his upper arm. 'Err, that's not right,' he said. Talk about an understatement.

If it had been me, I would've cried my eyes out. We had to stop off at the nearest service station, where he was picked up by an ambulance and taken to hospital. The injury ruled him out of the game and he'd also miss the final if we made it through.

It was a huge blow and we lost the first leg 2-1, but we won by the identical scoreline in the return fixture, which meant the game went to penalties. Jason Kennedy had scored two incredible goals in both legs, but his penalty was saved by Tommy Lee in the shootout. Luckily, it didn't matter, and it was left to Ben Muirhead, who had been in an older age group at Manchester United while I was there, to score the winning penalty. He was our fifth taker and smashed it straight down the middle to send us to Wembley. Rochdale hadn't experienced anything like it for years and it was great to see the town buzzing and getting behind us.

I had never been to Wembley before and was desperate to be involved. I'd been on the bench for both play-off matches, but on the morning of the game the gaffer pulled me aside after breakfast and said I wasn't going to be in the squad. I was gutted. Managers have to make tough decisions and someone has to be sacrificed, but that didn't make it any easier to swallow.

Stockport were our opponents in the final, and they had a quality team, which included the likes of Gary Dicker, Patrick Gleeson, Kevin Pilkington, Ashley Williams and Conrad Logan. Tommy Rowe, who was released by United at the same time as me, and for the exact same reason, also played that day. He'd really worked on the physical side of his game in the gym and had added muscle to his physique, which meant he could handle the physical demands of the division.

The final was a cracking game between two very good sides, but we lost 3-2. There were a lot of tears in the dressing room after the game, and I just wished I'd been on the pitch. The players who were chosen ahead of me didn't perform, and I felt I could have made an impact, but it's easy to say that when you're watching on.

Our heads were down, but Keith was adamant that we would get promoted the following season and told us to return for pre-season in four weeks' time. It didn't give us long to recharge the batteries, but we all knew it would give us a head start over our rivals. I was young, but the L plates were off and it was time to put my foot down.

Chapter 6
The missing piece

T HE sight of fresh meat went down well with one of the prisoners. 'Wit woo, haven't you brought a sort for us?' he shouted in my direction, as he was led through the grounds in handcuffs by a prison guard. I jumped back in my car, slammed the door shut and waited for help.

'Get out, you've got nothing to worry about,' laughed the man I'd come to meet. Guy Proctor was Rochdale's strength and conditioning coach, but he also worked as a personal trainer at Kirkham prison, near Blackpool. Every summer, he invited players to do weights sessions there to prepare us for the rigours of pre-season training. The gym was on the far side of the prison, which meant we had to walk past all the cells to reach it. I kept my head down as we walked through, but out of the corner of my eye I could see the inmates craning their necks out of their cell doors to see who was there.

I was escorted to the changing rooms by one of the guards. Once inside, I pulled on my t-shirt and shorts as quickly as possible. I'd seen plenty of films involving prisons and didn't fancy hanging about there naked for too long. There was no special treatment because we were footballers; we had to share the gym with the prisoners, who would spot us while we lifted heavy weights. At first I didn't dare speak to them, but I slowly plucked up the courage to ask them how they'd ended up behind bars.

One of the blokes was in his 20s and told me his story as I completed my fourth set on the bench press. He looked like a normal guy, but it turned out he'd been sentenced to life behind bars for murder. He'd seen red during an altercation with another man in his area and beat him to death with a concrete slab. I gulped and pushed out my remaining repetitions at speed. I didn't like the idea of getting on the wrong side of him while he was stood over me with a metal bar in his hands.

There was another man called Jimmy, who looked like he'd been born with a set of dumb-bells in his hands. He was 34 and had been in prison since he was 17, though I didn't dare ask him why. He must have been 6ft 5in tall and had the biggest set of lats I'd ever seen. He'd lifted that many weights his back looked like a triangle and his gigantic frame meant his head was tiny in comparison. I thought it would be funny to christen him 'Jimmy Pinhead' behind his back, but my attempts to make my team-mates laugh would come back to haunt me.

After a couple of weeks the prison didn't seem quite so daunting. We were on speaking terms with a few of the prisoners and they didn't mind us using their space, so long as we respected the gym and kept it tidy. 'Jimmy Pinhead' may as well have slept there, and his constant presence meant I could keep whispering his nickname to the lads and get a few cheap laughs at his expense. Before one of the sessions Jimmy approached me in the changing rooms with a menacing look on his face. 'Are you Joe Thompson?' he asked. 'No ... no, I've never heard of him,' I stuttered. 'Good,' he said. 'He's been calling me "Jimmy Pinhead"; if I find out you're lying, I'll make Mars Bars out of you.'

My heart was pounding. I fled out of the changing rooms and back to the safety of the gym. 'Lads, "Jimmy Pinhead" has just cornered me,' I said breathlessly. Guy, my team-mates and the rest of the prisoners burst out laughing, as did Jimmy, who had followed me back into the weights room. They'd all been in on the joke. Jimmy grabbed me by my neck and jokingly told me to never refer to him by that nickname ever again. I'd never been more relieved in my life and promised the lads I'd get them back eventually. The prison was a priceless experience and taught me not to judge a book by its cover. Don't get me wrong, some of them had committed some terrible crimes, but there were also some decent human beings in there who wanted to turn their lives around.

The prison was a world away from the freedom I'd experienced earlier that summer. Towards the end of the season, I'd split up with Lucy on the same day I passed my driving test. I thought girls loved guys with cars, but it turned out she'd had enough of playing second fiddle to football and my mischievous ways and decided it was time we went our separate ways. At the time I was gutted, but I wasn't down for long. I spent £3,500 on my first car, a Fiat Punto, which gave me the independence I craved, and then booked a summer holiday to Malia with a group of mates. I even managed to persuade my mum to let Reuben, who was only 16 and studying for his A-Levels, to come with me. He brought his books with him and revised during the day between our nights out on the strip.

We met up with another group of footballers who I knew from my time at Manchester United. Reece Brown, Danny Welbeck, Danny Drinkwater, Nicky Ajose, Scott Wooton, James Chester and Robbie Brady were staying at a hotel nearby and the two groups joined forces. There were 15 of us in total, and it was one of the best holidays I've ever had. We had a little bit of money, which meant we could stay somewhere half-decent and afford to rent quad bikes to explore the town. There were quite a few good-looking lads in the group and we had a great time letting our hair down and trying to chat up groups of girls. After the way the season had ended, it was the perfect way to switch off and forget about football.

Reaching the play-off final meant we only had four weeks off before we had to return for pre-season training. The work I'd done at the prison gym had paid off. I could see a subtle but definite difference in my physique, and mentally I felt refreshed. I was in the final year of my contract so I knew how important it was to put down a marker early on and cement a first-team place. Even as a youngster, the last year of your contract is a worrying time. All sorts of hypothetical situations entered my head. If I had a great season and then suffered a serious injury, would the club still offer me a contract, knowing that I could be out for nine months? What would happen if the season didn't go to plan and a new manager came in?

Politics also plays a part. Clubs will sometimes drop a player deliberately, regardless of his form, if he is about to activate a new contract but they have decided they don't want to keep him. One season, a team-mate of mine at Rochdale had played 24 games and needed just one more appearance to be awarded a new contract, only to be left out of the side for the final games of the campaign. He was at the back end of his career and the club felt it was time to balance the books and give a chance to a younger player on less money. It seemed unfair but football is a cruel business and smaller clubs have to make financially savvy decisions.

We went to Marbella for pre-season training, which was a welcome break from the day-to-day grind of the training ground. We got to see a bit of Puerto Banus and how the rich and famous lived, with their yachts and fast cars. The warm-weather training did us the world of good and we started the campaign on fire. We were top of the league for a while, ahead of Notts County, who had spent a lot of money hiring Sven-Goran Eriksson as their manager and bringing in the likes of Sol Campbell, Lee Hughes and Kasper Schmeichel on big wages. The nucleus of our team had been together for a while and there was a real connection between the lads, which showed on the pitch. In the tunnel, we weren't afraid to have a go at the opposition before kick-off to try and gain a psychological advantage. If one of our boys was fouled we'd loudly order each other to seek revenge on the offending player.

I love that side of the game and it's sad that it's slowly disappearing. On the pitch you can pretend to be as hard as you want because nothing serious is ever likely to happen. You have the safety net of a crowd, the referee and officials, so it's rare that trouble escalates beyond pushing and shoving. But there was one player I've faced who I always felt was capable of crossing the line. Over the years I've had numerous battles with Morecambe's Kevin Ellison. He's probably the biggest wind-up merchant in the Football League. He'll be 40 in February 2019 but still plays every week because he's kept himself in incredible shape. He's a good player, who has scored some brilliant goals, but he loves being the villain and getting in the face of the opposition. I've never seen a player use the crowd more to his advantage. He feeds off the hate of opposing fans and lifts his own supporters with his antics.

Our paths crossed early on that season when we faced Chester, who he was playing for at the time. He was sent off for violent conduct on the half-hour mark after head-butting one of our lads in an off-the-ball incident. 'JT, don't let him get away with that,' shouted one of our boys on the bench. Ellison's eyes were wide and he looked like a raging bull as he walked off the pitch. I decided to let him know I wasn't happy with him flattening my team-mate. He glared at me, with the veins popping on his shaven head, and told me he'd see me in the tunnel. I thought nothing of it, and scored our second goal in a 2-0 win, but at the end of the game he was there waiting for me. All hell broke loose as he tried to get to me through a crowd of bodies, but luckily my team-mates were on hand to stop him in his tracks. I'm not sure how I would've fared if he'd managed to get to me, but I probably wouldn't have emerged victorious.

It wasn't the only time that season that our team spirit helped us out of a tight corner. We were all on a night out at a student club in Manchester when one of the boys was punched in the face. In a matter of seconds it all kicked off. I was sat on a sofa and looked up to see all the boys wading in to protect those who were being attacked. I thought to myself, 'We're in it together here, we've got each other's backs.' I don't condone violence, particularly when there's alcohol involved, but the fact everyone stood up for each other spoke volumes. News of the incident got back to Keith Hill, who gave us a dressing down, but he was happy that we'd stuck together and made sure we all came away unscathed.

At that age I would go out on a Saturday night but it was rare that I drank. Most of the time I'd stick to soft drinks and be the taxi driver for my mates. I love music and sometimes it's nice to just go out after a game and unwind, particularly if adrenaline is still flowing through your veins. If you win 3-0 and there's music playing in the dressing room, it can quickly snowball into a night out. We'll start by going out for food and before you know it we've tried out a couple of bars and it's the early hours of the morning. I've always been mindful not to take the piss, though, because you have to be professional and make sure you keep yourself in tip-top shape.

Part of the reason we were such a tight-knit unit was because we had such a small squad, who had all got to know each other. But the lack of numbers meant we slowly started to run out of steam. Our style of football was physically demanding. Keith liked to play a pressing game and win the ball back high up the pitch. To do that you need to be able to sprint, repeatedly, for 90 minutes. Over the course of a season, particularly in the Football League when you're playing two games a week, that style takes its toll on your body. We didn't have the luxury of rotating players and a combination of fatigue and injuries curtailed our brilliant start.

We didn't manage to clinch automatic promotion to League One, but we still ended the 2008/09 season in sixth place, which meant we were in the play-offs for the second consecutive year. We played Gillingham in the semi-finals, but after a 0-0 draw in the first leg at Spotland, we lost 2-1 in the return fixture. It was gutting to come so close again, but on a personal note I'd made progress. I ended the season with 35 appearances and featured in both play-off games, having missed out altogether a year earlier. My efforts were rewarded with a new two-year deal, worth £700 a week, which would rise in my second year. I'd only just turned 20, so I felt like a millionaire compared to the money I'd been on as a YTS.

After breaking up with Lucy, I'd decided to be single for the following 12 months so that I could concentrate on football. I didn't want any distractions as I tried to win a new contract. My plan had worked, but around Christmas time the following season someone caught my eye. I'd been to a few house parties and kept seeing the same girl from afar. She looked different to the other girls; she was dark and, like me, clearly had mixed heritage. I kept tabs on her, so to speak, and the more I saw of her, the more I wanted to go over and chat, but it took a while before I plucked up the courage to approach her.

I eventually made my move during a night out at Circle nightclub in Manchester. She was sat on a sofa and I decided it was the perfect time to try and work my magic. I can't remember my exact words, but I walked over to her and said something like, 'Are you too cool to get up and dance?' Smooth, I know. I sat down next to her and we got chatting. Chantelle Perry was two years older than me and very independent. She was a self-employed hairdresser who was originally from Hull. She went back there three days a week to see various clients and already had her own apartment in Manchester. She let me know that she had already heard about me and my 'dickhead' group of footballers. Charming. I had a new challenge on my hands. I liked the fact that she had her head screwed on and already had her own flourishing career. She didn't need me, but I hoped, eventually, that she'd want me.

Our first date was at an Odeon cinema at the Printworks in Manchester. If the conversation was dead I knew we could just watch the film, but she caught me off guard by telling me to meet her early for some lunch. I'd already eaten after training and ordered a small portion of food. I barely touched it because I was so full and nervous. Aside from trying to impress her, I was also wary that we were going to the main cinema in the city centre.

I wanted to keep it low key and didn't want any mates to potentially see us together. She was calling the shots and told me we were going to watch *Avatar*. It was an animated film, so we both had to wear 3D glasses. I couldn't believe it; I thought she was this cool girl with a bit of an attitude and there she was watching a 12A film like a geek. Even worse, I could see my own reflection in her glasses; I was losing street cred by the minute.

We dated for four months between November and February and I soon realised I was falling for her. Neither of us were seeing other people and we made it official shortly after I'd turned 21 in March. She was keen to plan a summer holiday together, but firstly I wanted to concentrate on my football. Rochdale were third in the league and on course for promotion. The club hadn't been promoted in 35 years and I was having a good season, which I wanted to finish with a bang. In the event we went up, I was also guaranteed a £12,000 bonus, which would pay for a week-long trip to Las Vegas with a few of the lads.

After missing out on the play-offs twice, we were at last promoted to League One at the end of the 2009/10 season after holding on to third spot. I immediately put my extra cash towards Vegas. My team-mate Simon Ramsden told me he would book the flights and accommodation, having been there a couple of times before. 'Just bring your spends, I'll sort the rest,' he said. Joining us were two other Rochdale lads, Tom Kennedy and Sam Russell, as well as Dean Shiels, who was playing for Hibernian at the time. We all met at the airport, where Simon revealed he'd booked the trip for ten days, rather than the agreed seven. I couldn't believe he'd added an extra three days to the trip when he knew I hadn't been certain I could go until promotion had been secured. Even worse, he hadn't even sorted a hotel, which meant we'd have to find one when we landed. He shrugged his shoulders. 'It'll be right man,' he said in his Mackem accent.

We arrived on the Vegas strip, suitcases in hand. I was immediately caught up in the bright lights. 'Pick a hotel,' said

Simon. I was excited and suddenly loved the spontaneity of the trip. The hotel set us back about £700 and I then lost £600 in 20 minutes on a roulette machine inside the lobby while the lads checked in. I had a Thomas Cook bag stuffed with notes but I soon realised it wasn't going to be enough. At one point, my bank called to notify me about large transactions on my account from Vegas cash machines. I assured them it was me and made sure there was plenty left for me to withdraw. We didn't do much sightseeing. There were no trips to the Grand Canyon or any other landmarks. Most of our time was spent at pool parties and in nightclubs. It was a relentless holiday and after one particularly heavy night an old woman had to make sure I got in a lift and went back to my room at 4am. 'That's enough for you,' she said, after her own night-long stint on the slot machines. It was the first time I'd drunk properly and it had taken its toll.

After four days, we all sat down in the hotel and looked at each other through bleary eyes. 'Lads, should we get an early flight home?' said Tom Kennedy. Everyone was in agreement that we should book a flight for the following day. Vegas had physically and financially destroyed us and we couldn't handle another five days of partying. I called Chantelle and told her I was coming home early. She'd been to Vegas herself and knew I wouldn't last the full ten days. Once again, she was one step ahead of me. I'd had a lot of fun in Vegas and the previous summer in Malia, but inwardly I knew that I needed an anchor in my life. When I came home we decided to make our relationship concrete and then went on our first holiday to Dubai.

We'd only been together for six months but going away felt right. Our backgrounds were similar in the sense that neither of us had had the perfect childhood. Chantelle's father committed suicide when her mum was pregnant with her, which meant she was brought up by her step4dad, Paul. She knew from a young age he wasn't her real dad, but he was in everything but blood. It takes a brave man to bring up someone else's child and it was probably even more difficult given that Paul was white and Chantelle was mixed race, which meant he got funny looks wherever they went together. He loved her like she was his own and gave her stability as she grew up in a settled family unit.

At the time, I was still living at home and my relationship with my mum grew increasingly strained. We fell out over the smallest of things and I'd go and stay with my auntie. A few days later we'd make up and I'd be back in my bedroom with my brother. Over the course of the next year, I spent an increasing amount of time at Chantelle's apartment by Deansgate Locks. At first she didn't come to any of my games, but after a while she started to attend the odd one and I also introduced her to my mum. When I was with Lucy, I felt my mum was worried that I'd be spoilt by her parents and perhaps change in some way, but she got on well with Chantelle from the start. She recognised that she was her own girl and didn't dote on me.

I was keen to settle down and I understand why managers want players to find themselves a solid partner as soon as possible, because they don't want you to have too much time on your hands. If you're single and you get home from training at 2pm, the first thing you do is ring your mates or a girl that you're seeing to find out what they're up to. Your manager wants you to have your feet up resting but instead you're driving around in your car and wasting your energy on other things. A lot of players end up settling down very young because of that external pressure, but for others it's a difficult thing to do because they want to socialise and have different experiences.

When you're a young footballer, finding the right girl is easier said than done. When you go to certain nightclubs, you know there will be girls who are there with the sole intention of trying to find a footballer. I've seen plenty of young lads get with girls who have wanted them more for their wealth than their personalities. Further down the line they've seen their true colours, but by that point it's been too late because they've got a house or had a child, which has led to a complex and expensive divorce. Seeing those sorts of things can make you paranoid, but I was fortunate to have met someone genuine, who had little interest in footballers or what I did for a living.

I'd only been with Chantelle for about 12 months when we bought our first house together. The lease on her apartment was due to expire and we both felt ready to take our relationship to the next step. We found a three-bedroom property in Prestwich, on the outskirts of Manchester. It was on a new estate full of young couples who were all buying their first homes. The area was the perfect balance between city and country life. We were only a 10- or 15-minute drive from the city centre and the same distance from my mum and auntie. It was better for me to be a little bit away from town so I didn't have the temptations of bars and nightclubs on my doorstep. I was also happy to put a bit of space between me and Rochdale. Living close to the ground is great when you're winning and fans are patting you on the back, but if you're not playing well they want to know why when they see you buying a pint of milk in the shop.

Without realising it, I'd started a new chapter in my life. I was 21, had bought my first home with a girl that I loved and made a good start to life in League One. Little did I know, another one was about to follow.

Chapter 7

A man's world

I T was the height of summer, but winds of change were sweeping over my world. The sweat and toil of the first day of pre-season training was the same, but the sights and sounds were very different. In June 2011, after four successful years at Rochdale, Keith Hill had left to take charge of Championship side Barnsley, and taken his right-hand man David Flitcroft with him.

Since the age of 17, his barking voice had been the soundtrack to my working week but now it had been replaced with the softer tones of Steve Eyre. On paper, his pedigree was first class. He'd previously been a youth-team coach at Manchester City and helped to bring through a talented group of players, including Micah Richards, Ishmaël Miller and Kelvin Etuhu, but this was his first managerial role at senior level.

I couldn't fault his credentials as a coach, but dealing with grown men is a completely different challenge to working with teenage boys. He was a perfectly good bloke but preferred a kid gloves approach, when the squad of players he'd inherited had thrived on tough love. When older players questioned his decisions, he struggled to stand up to them and it was often left to his assistant, Frankie Bunn, to act as his voice.

From his early days in charge it became obvious the appointment was a bad fit. On the training ground and in the dressing room he struggled to communicate when senior players questioned his methods. In training, he preferred structured drills, involving lots of cones and crossing drills, which was like something out of an FA coaching manual, whereas Keith always tailored his sessions to a game scenario, which the lads enjoyed.

Steve's recruitment also left a lot to be desired. We'd finished the previous season in ninth place, three points short of the play-offs, which was a brilliant achievement in our first campaign back in League One. But the current side had been together for a long time and everyone knew we would need an injection of fresh blood to maintain our progress. New faces did arrive, but they lacked the quality to improve the squad and it was the start of a reversal in our fortunes.

Still, on that first day of pre-season training, I was desperate to impress. Steve had spoken to me at great length about his plans and I'd put in a lot of effort over the summer to ensure I made a good first impression, only for a freak injury to ruin all my hard work. On the first day we went through a light warm-up before doing a series of sprints, but midway through the opening run my back went into spasm, leaving me in agony on the grass.

The physio came running over, but my back was locked and I could barely walk or stand up straight. 'Fucking hell,' I thought. It was the worst possible start and I feared I'd suffered a long-term injury. It turned out I was right. I'd torn a disc in my lower lumbar and my back had gone into spasm as a defence mechanism to prevent further damage. I was told it's an injury that can happen to anyone at any time and that it would take at least two weeks before I could even stand up properly.

We were due to go away to Marbella again for warm-weather training and the coaching staff agreed it was best for me to join the rest of the squad and try and do some light rehabilitation work in the warm weather. Fortunately, the temperatures seemed to loosen up my back and by the end of the two weeks I was able to do some gentle running in straight lines. It was the first time I'd suffered a serious injury and made me realise how your body works as a chain. A problem in an isolated area incapacitates so many other muscle groups.

It was two months later, in August, when I was finally ready to return, but I faced a fight for a regular starting place. I featured in pretty much every game between August and October, but I often started on the bench and was slowly growing frustrated at my lack of playing time. It was around this time that my agent received a phone call offering me an escape route. Keith was keen to take me to Barnsley on loan and wanted to know if I was 100 per cent fit. I told him I was and felt excited by the possibility of testing myself in the Championship, a level I felt I was more than capable of competing at.

The deal was agreed, but yet another injury setback scuppered the move. The day before I was due to join Barnsley, I tore my left quadriceps muscle as I pulled my leg back to take a shot at goal in a Football League Trophy tie against Walsall. I was forced to come off at half-time and then faced another two months on the sidelines. It was a nightmare start to the season, and by the time I was fit again in early January Steve had been sacked, with Rochdale languishing in the relegation places, four points adrift of safety.

Rochdale's youth-team manager, Chris Beech, was placed in temporary charge. Beechy had been my manager before I progressed to the first team and was similar to Steve in that his experience had been forged in youth coaching. However, he'd had a good career in the Football League and that showed in his sessions. He was very professional and able to walk us through exactly what we needed to do because he could still play. There are some brilliant managers who haven't had great playing careers, but I have an instant respect for someone who can do what he's asking of the players.

Unfortunately for Chris, his spell in charge was never likely to be made permanent. In late January, after a winless run of six matches, Accrington Stanley boss John Coleman and his assistant, Jimmy Bell, were given the job of saving us from relegation.

John's appointment was a coup at the time; he was the longest-serving manager in the Football League, having been at the Crown Ground for 13 years. Only Sir Alex Ferguson and Arsene Wenger had lasted longer than him at the helm of an English club.

John and Jimmy could easily have been a comedy double act. They were both scousers and bounced off each other incredibly well. The sheer force of their personalities brought a fun factor to training and lifted the spirits of everyone at the club. Most managers and coaches stay away from the dressing room and regard it as the players' inner sanctum, but not those two – they were everywhere, and loved being amongst the banter. They'd join in with five-a-side games and deliberately make controversial refereeing decisions to see how we'd react. Once training was finished, they'd crack jokes at someone's expense and then revel in their embarrassment.

Their training sessions weren't as professional as I'd been used to, but their bizarre methods had obviously worked elsewhere. There was one occasion when John took the whole squad to Southport beach to do a running session, but there didn't seem to be any clear goal behind what we were doing. He'd tell us to run to a tree in the distance and back to the starting point in five minutes, or another time he'd plucked from thin air. It soon became obvious that the idea was just to run us until we were physically exhausted. One thing they did have was an unbelievable passion for football and a win-at-all-costs mentality.

There was a feel-good factor around the place again, but even John's unique methods weren't enough to stem the tide of bad results. Our biggest problem was scoring goals, and he wasn't able to sign someone who could give us an extra cutting edge in the final third. We put up a bit of a fight in the final months of the season with a win over local rivals Oldham and a thrilling 3-3 draw against Exeter. I scored our third goal in that game, which I thought would be the winner, with a little lob over the goalkeeper, only for them to peg us back in the dying seconds. Relegation back to League Two was confirmed in April following a 2-1 defeat at Chesterfield.

On a personal note, I was frustrated to have barely contributed to the fight. After recovering from my quadriceps injury I began to struggle with the same muscle in the opposite leg. Imbalances in strength often occur when you suffer an injury and it was a problem that kept me on the sidelines yet again. I was desperate to show John and Jimmy what I was capable of and felt helpless sat in the stands. I only really featured in the final six weeks of the season, by which time our fate was already decided.

It had taken years of hard work and perseverance to reach League One, and I was gutted to see it all unravel. My contract expired at the end of the season and I had a big decision to make regarding my future. I was 24, which meant I couldn't leave on a free transfer, and Rochdale could still demand a substantial compensation fee from any team who wished to sign me. Relegation had cost us an estimated £500,000 but we'd been run diligently by our chairman Chris Dunphy and weren't in any danger of financial meltdown. The target for the following season would be promotion.

Rochdale's ambition matched my own, but I told John that I didn't want to commit to a deal until I saw who the club brought in over the summer. I wanted to see if we would bring in the right quality, and despite the offer of a new contract I still wasn't 100 per cent convinced John fancied me. In the meantime, I was given a week-to-week deal on the same terms of my previous contract, while my agent kept his ear to the ground for any interest from other clubs.

It was around this time that I started working with a psychologist, Martin Robin Hall. I was disappointed I hadn't kicked on despite doing everything right in training and in the gym, and I wanted to see if I could improve my performance by tapping into the power of the mind. Some of the world's best athletes use psychologists to learn how to deal with the pressure of elite performance, and I was curious to see if it could give me an edge on the pitch.

On average, I see him about four times a year and he's become a bit of a mentor, who not only gives me advice about the psychological side of my game, but life as well. My only regret is that normally I seek his help when things have started to go badly. In hindsight, I think it's best to have progressive chats when you're on top of your game so you can see what you're doing right and prolong your purple patch.

During one of our sessions we started talking about where I wanted to go and what I thought I could achieve in the game. I told him I'd had a premonition for some time of me walking around a pitch after a game, wearing a blue shirt and white Nike Vapors, while carrying a little boy on my shoulders. I didn't know where this vision came from or the success it perhaps alluded to, but Martin told me to keep hold of it and use it as a goal to pursue.

Unfortunately, he couldn't help me make up my mind about my future, but five weeks into pre-season training a tempting offer presented itself. I played in a friendly against Hull and then scored against Blackburn Rovers at Ewood Park.

Tranmere Rovers manager Ronnie Moore was sat in the stands and I saw him speaking to a few Rochdale officials after the game. A day or so later they lodged a £100,000 bid, which was broken down into a £50,000 lump sum and two instalments of £25,000. The contract they put in front of me was a two-year deal worth £1,200 a week, plus bonuses.

Ronnie told me he wanted to get me in the building as quickly as possible, and I was keen to stay in League One and test myself at a bigger club. Prenton Park could hold over 16,000 people and they had a loyal, passionate fanbase. In January I'd also found out that Chantelle was pregnant with our first child and I knew the additional money would give us more financial stability over the next two years. Ten days before the start of the new season, I put pen to paper and waved goodbye to Rochdale after eight years at the club. It was sad to move on but I had to satisfy my ambition and see how far I could go.

On my first day at Tranmere I felt like the new kid at St Vincent's Primary School all over again. My nerves were jangling as I drove into training to meet my new team-mates. It was a very different environment to what I'd been used to at Rochdale. The dressing room was full of strong characters and big egos, which had been built around a core of players who had been released by north-west clubs like Liverpool, Everton and Wigan. One of the main men was Ian Goodison. He was a club legend, who had been there for over eight years and won over 100 caps for Jamaica. Andy Robinson was another alpha male and a vocal guy who you could hear from a mile away. He'd played for the club's academy as a kid and had spells at Swansea and Leeds United before returning to Birkenhead.

It was difficult trying to find my place in the food chain. There wasn't the same team spirit that we'd had at Rochdale and it often felt like it was every man for himself. When you join a new club, you face a dilemma over whether to just be yourself or go in there and put on a confident front so nobody tries to take the piss. Looking back, I was probably somewhere between the two. I certainly wasn't myself. That didn't mean I didn't make friends, though. I felt at ease around the younger players in the squad and quickly became good mates with a young midfielder called Max Power. Like me, he was set to become a father for the first time and we found common ground over the complaints of our respective girlfriends during their pregnancies.

I was relishing the challenge of winning the respect of my new team-mates and fans, but a few days before the start of the new season a strange rash appeared on my face. At first I thought it was a shaving cut but slowly it started to grow. My doctor suspected it was impetigo and prescribed me a course of antibiotics, but still it continued to spread. It wasn't something that affected my football, but mentally it knocked my confidence. When you're on the pitch, players are never shy of pointing out any sort of physical deficiency in an attempt to get in your head, and it's something I would often do to put an opponent off his game. It took a few months to clear up and I was relieved it turned out to be nothing sinister.

For all of my concerns over our dressing room, we began the campaign with a ten-match unbeaten run. I started pretty much every game and felt I did myself justice. Off the pitch, Chantelle was due to give birth on 10 September but we were taken by surprise ten days early. Ronnie had rested me for a game against Colchester United, so I put the time off to good use, if you know what I mean. After we'd gone to bed, she woke up in the middle of the night in pain. Our first child had grown impatient and was ready to enter our world. We were caught so off guard we hadn't even packed an overnight bag, and I drove us as fast as possible to Manchester North Hospital. We must've done a 20-minute journey in about five minutes.

Chantelle's labour lasted eight hours. I remember looking at her neck; there were veins popping everywhere. This 5ft 5in woman had turned into the Incredible Hulk as she pushed our baby out. At 11:23am on the morning of 1 September 2012, Thailulah Lily Thompson was born. We call her Lula, but we decided on her full name because we had to cancel a holiday we'd booked to Thailand after learning of Chantelle's pregnancy, which meant she couldn't have any of the injections she needed when you visit Asia. I picked her up and took a long look at her; she was my double. In that moment, the next 20 years of her life flashed by like a film reel in my head. I imagined her riding her first bike, going to her high school prom, taking her to her first date with her boyfriend, graduation, marriage.

It was the happiest moment of my life, but when Chantelle told me she was pregnant nine months earlier I was excited and scared at the same time. I was 22, but a young 22. Everything had happened so quickly; we'd met, bought a house and were expecting our first child all in the space of 18 months.

Chantelle was older and comfortable with it, but I questioned whether I was ready for the responsibility. I wasn't sure if I'd done enough and learnt enough about myself as a young man to be a good father.

On top of that, I'd been worried about fitting in at a new club, but thankfully my concerns soon evaporated and I loved going to the antenatal classes and buying clothes ready for Lula's arrival. We wanted to be able to prepare properly for the birth and so we'd made the decision to find out the sex of the baby before she was born. I didn't mind whether it was a boy or a girl and I started to imagine what she would look and sound like when she eventually arrived.

We were lucky that Lula was a good baby and adapted to a routine very quickly. She began breastfeeding immediately, which meant I was spared the task of doing any bottle feeds in the middle of the night for the first few months. She also moved from her Moses basket and into a cot within about eight weeks and not long after she was sleeping all through the night.

Some high-profile footballers hire nannies to look after their children so they can get enough rest, but even if money was no object I would never have entertained doing that. Those early months in a child's life are magical and you can never get them back. As a parent it is your duty to shape their life and I'm not sure you can do that properly if you're only playing a part-time role in bringing them up. I loved rolling my sleeves up and doing the nappy changing and playing games with her as she got a bit older.

My happiness at becoming a father made it even more difficult for me to understand my dad's absence from my own childhood. I was younger than he was when mum gave birth to me, but he still found it impossible to stop hanging around with his mates and curtailing the carefree lifestyle he'd enjoyed in his teens and early 20s. I know a few footballers who, like him, have struggled to adapt to fatherhood. They finish training and go home and play FIFA on their Xbox and leave the childcare stuff to their girlfriend or wife. I understand that you have to be selfish as a footballer, but that excuse only stretches so far.

Chantelle was incredible throughout. During her pregnancy, she continued to work until one month before she gave birth and somehow still found the energy to do things at home to prepare for Lula's arrival. I remember her pestering me about painting the nursery, but I kept making excuses about being too tired. One afternoon I came home to find her stood on a chair painting and angrily pointing her brush at me between strokes. She took to motherhood like a duck to water and seeing her with Lula only intensified the love I already felt for her. My two girls were my absolute world and suddenly I felt like I didn't really matter anymore. As long as they were happy and healthy, I felt content.

On the pitch, we continued to blow away the rest of League One. At Christmas we were top of the division and performing far better than anyone had predicted. Even the players were surprised by how well we were doing. In January we signed Ben Gibson from York City. His personality was black and white and he was a breath of fresh air. He's a typical north-east lad and one of the most down-to-earth guys I've ever met. He fitted in with the rest of the dressing room immediately because he didn't pretend to be anything other than himself. It takes a lot of courage to let your guard down when you move to a new club, and, in hindsight, I wish I'd done the same thing and then maybe I would've felt more of a part of the team. Despite playing a lot of football in the first half of the season, I still felt like an outsider.

Given our lack of team spirit, I always felt like we had a self-destruct button, which would be triggered in the event we hit a rough patch. I hoped I'd be proven wrong, but after amassing 50 points in the first half of the season we struggled to get another 20 after that. Shortly after the New Year, I fell out of favour with Ronnie and decided to return to Rochdale in March, on a short-term loan deal, until the end of the season.

Keith was back in charge following the sacking of John Coleman in January and had contacted my agent to see if I was open to the idea of going back. It was an easy decision to make, but in typical Keith fashion he gave me a verbal dig to make sure I put pen to paper. 'Do you want to actually play football or just pretend you're a footballer and sit at home playing families?' he asked me over the phone. A lot had changed since we'd last met, but clearly the terms of our relationship hadn't.

Rochdale were struggling in League One and I was determined to make sure they didn't suffer back-to-back relegations. Keith threw me straight into the starting line-up and I'd played seven games when Tranmere suddenly recalled me in April. They had an injury crisis and Ronnie needed bodies immediately, so I reluctantly headed back, though I at least felt I'd now be certain of a run of games. Keith disagreed. 'Ronnie wants you back, but after next week's game you'll be back in the stands,' he whispered in my ear. It was classic Keith, he was looking out for me and wanted me to understand the reality of the situation, but I knew full well that he was also sowing seeds of doubt in my head so I'd be keen to go back again in the event that happened. It turned out that he was right. I spent the rest of the season making brief cameo appearances from the bench. We finished in 11th place, which was certainly no disgrace, but I wasn't happy with my efforts. I felt I hadn't done myself justice or showed the supporters why I'd been signed. Tranmere fans know their football and I wanted to prove to them that I was a good player.

Over the summer I went away to Portugal for a week or so and took stock of the past 12 months. We stayed at a resort in Vilamoura, which I'd been to before with Lucy and her family. My mum, as well as Chantelle's mum and dad, came along with us, and I felt like a tour guide as I showed them the best parts of the marina. Chantelle's parents wondered how I'd amassed such a detailed knowledge of the local area in the space of a few short hours, but I kept the source of my information a secret.

I gave my image a reboot by growing my hair longer and getting a high-top haircut, so I looked a bit like Will Smith in *The Fresh Prince of Bel-Air*. I guess I wanted to refresh myself psychologically with a new look. Bold haircuts and fancy boots can be a big risk, because you put yourself above the parapet to be shot at if you don't perform. But if you do, it can work to your advantage, because people will say, 'did you see the guy with the yellow boots or the haircut?' I was keen to stand out from the crowd, but something else would do that for me.

Chapter 8
The darkest hour

IT was a sweltering hot August day, the sort that footballers dread when they draw back their curtains on a Saturday morning. We were playing Crewe away. Tranmere fans had travelled in their numbers and we were doing our warm-up in front of the away end, but I already felt like the tank was empty. My throat was parched and my thoughts and movements were sluggish when they ought to have been razor sharp. Something wasn't quite right.

My pre-match routine had been perfect, which made my lethargy all the more unusual. Every player has one, designed to banish some imaginary force that could somehow affect his performance.

From Thursday night onwards, my focus is purely on football as I shut the engines down ahead of the game. If Lula is doing something at school, Chantelle will attend and also drop her off on the Friday morning. The day before a match I do as little as possible in training and never do shooting practice. I don't want to peak too soon or go into the game thinking I can't hit a barn door.

The night before, I eat dinner at 7pm. My meal, before I turned vegan, was normally chicken and pasta and I'd be in bed by 10pm. Chantelle has always worked Saturdays so her mum would pick Lula up and look after her until the Sunday afternoon. That meant I had the house to myself on the morning of the game. I'd have a big bowl of porridge with loads of fruit, raspberries and linseeds, washed down with green juice. This was followed by scrambled eggs on brown toast with avocado and spinach. My pre-match meal, three hours before the game, would be Friday's leftovers.

It probably sounds like an obsessive routine, but it meant that I knew after Thursday night I had no excuses. If I did well it was because I'd done everything right. If I had a shocker, but had done everything right off the pitch, then I could narrow down what had gone wrong. Maybe it was how I warmed up or perhaps my opponent had just got the better of me on the day. You have to be very selfish, but even before Lula was born I set my stall out with Chantelle and told her this was how I had to live. To this day she'll pester me to do certain things, but I tell her that I have to stick to my routine. If you cut corners in professional football you'll get caught out.

Everything was in place that Saturday afternoon, but when the game kicked off I felt like I was being tossed around in a tumble dryer for the first 20 minutes. Everyone seemed to be moving at a million miles per hour. The roar of the crowd and the players on the pitch were just a blur of noise and colour. I felt like I was running in quicksand and playing in slow motion. I was taken by surprise by players tackling me and didn't have the speed of thought to make quick decisions.

I thought that I was just having one of those unexplainable starts to a game when your lungs and legs are burning before you settle into the rhythm of the match and get your second wind. But my condition didn't seem to change. Twenty minutes in, our right-back, Danny Holmes, was sent off and I was substituted as Keith made a tactical switch. For the first time in my life I was relieved to be coming off the pitch. I'd dodged a bullet. I felt terrible and described my symptoms to our club doctor, but he didn't think there was any immediate cause for concern and told me to rest up and get plenty of fluids in my system.

In the weeks before that afternoon, my physical and mental state had never been better. During the summer I'd really focused on nutrition and what I thought was a healthy diet at that time. Tranmere had employed a nutritionist who looked at our calorie intake and how it was broken down into carbohydrates, protein and fat and then liaised with our fitness coach, so that training and food intake were in sync. Our sessions became shorter but were more game specific, including lots of sprint work, which was perfect for my style of play.

During a pre-season match against Camel Laird, a non-league side who the club face every summer, we ran riot in a 7-1 win. The margin of victory was unsurprising given the gulf in quality between the sides, but on a personal level I knew the additional detail to my training had improved me physically. I scored a volley and set two goals up that day for our new signing, Ryan Lowe. He was an experienced striker, small and slight in build, and a bit of a poacher in the mould of Francis Jeffers. He saw that I could be a useful source of ammunition for him in front of goal, so we immediately hit it off.

We played Burnley in another pre-season game and my performance earned the praise of our coach, John McMahon. His endorsement and the consistency of my performances were building blocks for my confidence. My form continued when the season got underway. In a Johnstone's Paint Trophy game against Mansfield, I was up against a right-back called James Jennings. He'd been at Macclesfield when I was in Rochdale's youth team and I gave him the run-around on the night and let him know about it. If I'm having a good game I've got a bit of a gob on me and I like to let the man I'm up against know that I'm coming for him, just like I did when I was pretending to be Ian Wright and Thierry Henry as a kid.

That game was the first time I'd been named man of the match in a home fixture for Tranmere, and I felt it took the heat off me a bit. Their fans hadn't seen the best of me at Prenton Park and it was my first step towards showing them why I'd been signed. My tail was up and I was man of the match again when Crawley came to town. One of my good friends, Nicky Adams, who I'd played alongside at Rochdale, was playing on the left wing. We were represented by the same agent, so Lloydy was sat in the stands with divided loyalties. The night before the game I spoke to Nicky on the phone and had a bit of banter, but once the referee blew his whistle the goodwill went out of the window.

We went 1-0 down early on, but I scored twice to turn the game around in the first half. One of those goals came after the goalkeeper had miskicked the ball and was left stranded miles out of his goal. I ran the full length of the half and rounded him before slotting it home. It was the sort of situation where if you're not confident you can easily make a mess of it because you've got so much time on your hands. But I was flying and there was never a doubt in my mind that I was going to score. For the rest of the match the pressure was off me; I'd done my job, which enabled me to play with freedom. Once again, I was dishing out the verbals and even tried winding Nicky up by telling him he wasn't giving his full-back enough help defensively.

In the end my cockiness came back to haunt me. The game finished 3-3 and I was denied a hat-trick after a block on the goal line, but I'd done enough to be named man of the match for a second time, which was a small consolation. I was over the moon at the start I'd made to the season, but then everything suddenly came grinding to a halt. After my nightmare at Crewe, my symptoms would come and go, but a few weeks later I suffered a repeat episode of what had happened at Gresty Road in a home game against Port Vale. Once again, the pace felt relentless and I was all over the place. Remarkably, we again went down to ten men in the first half and I was sacrificed. I deserved to be brought off but there wasn't much I could do about it; inwardly something was sapping me of my energy.

A few days after the game the whole squad had taken part in a hot yoga session to help us loosen up and speed up our recovery. For some reason I just couldn't reach one of the positions, which required me to lift my arms above my head. I was in pain as I tried and failed to perform the move and was shocked to feel a load of lumps in my armpit. I alerted the club doctor again and he decided to send me off for further tests. I was pretty certain I was suffering with a bout of glandular fever. Reuben had come down with it during his freshers' week at university after getting with too many girls, and the symptoms I was feeling seemed to tally with his.

But my condition continued to worsen. I was losing weight and constantly felt tired. I then started to have night sweats and I'm not talking about the sort you have when you've got a fever. One night I woke up at 2am and literally felt like someone had thrown a bottle of water over me and Chantelle. The bed was like a swimming pool and the sheets and duvet were completely soaked. My temperature was fluctuating between roasting hot and freezing cold and I had horrendous pain in my neck. I'd had enough and was booked in for a biopsy to find out once and for all what was going on. My team-mate, Ash Taylor, had undergone the same procedure and thought I probably just had a cyst. I hoped he was right.

I was pencilled in for an early morning appointment at a hospital on the Wirral. The night before I stayed at my team-mate Evan Horwood's house. He's a cracking lad from the north-east, with a wand of a left peg. He'd joined us from Hartlepool that summer and lived pretty close to the surgery, which saved me the hassle of having to get up at the crack of dawn and drive there from Manchester. I remember being sat in his house refusing to take my jacket off. 'Is my house too cold for you or something?' he asked. I knew the heating was on and that it was perfectly warm but I was freezing cold and felt like I was sat outside in the middle of winter.

The following morning he dropped me off at the surgery. The nurse injected me with anesthetic to send me to sleep, but after she had counted down from ten to one, I was still awake and my hand started to swell in size. Another nurse intervened and jabbed me with a needle, which knocked me out cold. When I came round, the first thing I looked at was my hand, which had thankfully returned to its normal size. I had three stitches in my neck from the biopsy and was told I'd have my results in two to three weeks. I jumped back on a train to Manchester, where Chantelle was waiting for me at the station. We set off back home and began the wait for the news.

Wednesday, 23 October 2013 will be etched on to my psyche for the rest of my life. That was the date, two weeks later, when I was asked to return to the surgery to discuss my results. Me and Chantelle decided to make a day of it while we were there and brought Lula along with us. I imagined I'd be in and out in 10 or 15 minutes so we could go to the beach afterwards, have a bit of dinner somewhere and a look around the shops. The three of us were called into Professor Radford's office, who was an elderly gentleman with a comforting voice. 'Do you want the good news or the bad news?' he asked me. 'Let's start with the bad news,' I replied. 'The bad news is you've got cancer,' he said. 'The good news is that it's Hodgkin Lymphoma, which is treatable.'

I was dumbfounded. My heart and mind were racing as I tried to digest the news. A thousand questions raced around my head. It couldn't be right. The results must've been wrong.

I was only 23 and in the shape of my life. I looked at Chantelle and we both started crying. I wanted her to say something to make everything better but I knew there was nothing she could do. Professor Radford explained that Hodgkin Lymphoma was cancer of the blood. Tumours had formed on my lymph nodes; small, bean-sized noodles of tissue that form part of the immune system. The biopsy had uncovered an area the size of a watermelon on my chest covered in tumours, which meant hundreds upon hundreds of them were swimming around my body attacking my healthy cells.

Worse still, my cancer was categorised as stage 3S. This meant it was already well advanced and had reached my spleen, one of the body's key defences against illness. I would have to undergo 12 cycles of chemotherapy, one every two weeks, for six months, to try and rid my body of tumours. Each cycle would involve me spending a day or a day and a half in hospital, depending on how I'd reacted to the treatment. In my head I started to calculate the dates and naively thought I might be able to finish chemo and start training again by May or June. Professor Radford's response was firm. My season was over and there was no guarantee I'd play again, never mind at League One level.

We left his office, got in the car and set off back home. It was the worst journey of my life. It had been a sunny day, but rain began lashing down and bouncing off the windscreen. We then got stuck in traffic, while Lula was kicking and screaming in the back of the car. It was only just over a month since we'd celebrated her first birthday with a big party, and now in my darkest thoughts I was wondering if I'd be alive to see her second. Me and Chantelle stared outside at the gridlocked roads with tears rolling down our faces. We just wanted to get home and start doing some more research. I was inconsolable. I wasn't angry; I was more frustrated and felt that everything was so unfair. Why me? What had I done to deserve this? My lifestyle was perfect but even that hadn't been enough to protect me.

I didn't know how I was going to break the news to family and friends. My biggest concern was my mum. Stressful situations can trigger her bipolar disorder and send her off the rails. My brother was also living and working in Newcastle, so I knew he would feel helpless. They were the first people I told, while Chantelle spoke to her mum and dad. I then rang my agent, Lloydy, who took the news the worst out of everyone. The transfer market was shut, so he was in Abu Dhabi enjoying a well-earned holiday with his family. When I called, he was running along the beach in the sunshine, but minutes later I could hear him crying down the phone. Later on that day, his ten-year-old daughter found him under his duvet in bed bawling his eyes out. Looking back, I feel guilty that she had to see her dad in that state while they were supposed to be making happy memories.

Football was the last thing on my mind, but I needed to break the news to Tranmere. Lloydy had spoken to the club's chief executive to explain my situation and he'd relayed his message to the coaching staff. It took two days before Ronnie called me. I was surprised he didn't ring immediately, but I suppose he didn't quite know what to say and was probably trying to put things in place to replace me, knowing that I was unlikely to be kicking a ball again anytime soon. He told me to give him a call anytime if I needed 'a bit of Ronnie love'. I thought to myself, 'I'll need a bit more than that.' I was scared to think about the future. I was out of contract at the end of the season and had a mortgage to pay. Lloydy promised me we'd sit down with the PFA and draw up plans in the event I couldn't play again.

In the weeks that followed I underwent a multitude of tests and scans to establish baseline scores of my body's performance so my progress could be monitored. Although I'd only fallen ill a few weeks before, I was astonished to hear that I'd probably had the disease for up to three years. Professor Radford explained that his estimation was based on the size of the tumours and their current rate of growth, which could be used to predict when they had first formed. In a way, my fitness had counted against me. Because I was strong and healthy, my body had adapted and actively fought the cancerous cells. Had I been weaker, I'd probably have experienced the symptoms far sooner and been diagnosed with cancer when I was 21 or 22.

I started to rewind previous injuries and illnesses in my head and suddenly all the pieces of the puzzle started to fall into place. I lived an athlete's lifestyle, but little coughs and colds had always taken a little bit longer to shift. The previous season I'd picked up a dead leg during an indoor training match, an injury that normally takes no more than a week to clear up. Strangely, the pain in my leg just wouldn't budge, but our physio, Greg Blundell, was adamant that there was nothing wrong with me. He was under pressure from Ronnie to get me back on the pitch and from the outside couldn't see anything untoward. Greg is a top physio who treats his players' bodies like top-of-the-range sports cars and he'll do anything and everything to get them fit for a Saturday afternoon. I trusted his word, but my body told me otherwise.

There were other problems, like my thigh injury during my final season at Rochdale, which had taken far longer to heal than it should've done. I'd always assumed that I was just a slow healer, but I've since learned that when your body is dealing with cancer, it doesn't treat other injuries as a priority because it's concerned with waging an internal war with the cancerous cells attacking your body. Another incident also stood out from pre-season when I'd fainted after a dizzy spell during training. Again, I attributed that to dehydration and pushing myself too hard, but now I'm convinced it was my body slowly wilting against the tide of cancerous tumours.

I was at my lowest ebb, but I'd been encouraged by some of the statistics Professor Radford had told me regarding the survival rates of patients with Hodgkin Lymphoma. Based on 8,000 cases between 1988 and 2001, the five-year survival rate for people classified as stage three is 80 per cent. That means five years after the initial diagnosis, most sufferers are still alive and living with the disease. Given my age and the fact the cancer hadn't attacked one specific organ, he was optimistic my treatment would be a success, though he couldn't guarantee I'd be one of the lucky ones. Every case is individual and a whole host of factors can influence how your body deals with cancer and how intense your treatment will need to be.

I was desperate to get my treatment underway immediately, but I had to wait six weeks before it started. I went back and forth to the hospital for further tests but there didn't seem to be any urgency to get the ball rolling. I couldn't believe that something was killing me and still nothing was being done about it. I felt like a sitting duck being shot at. While the wait continued, my condition worsened. I had an idea of some of the problems I could encounter, but cancer is a sly disease and the symptoms creep up on you when you least expect it. Several weeks after my diagnosis I woke up in the middle of the night and couldn't breathe. I felt like a snake was slowly wrapping itself around my neck, tighter and tighter, before letting go and leaving me gulping in as much oxygen as possible. I panicked and called the club doctor, but he assured me I'd be fine and encouraged me to try and stay as calm as possible.

I was in limbo and tried to keep myself busy to occupy my mind and avoid dwelling on negative thoughts. My mood was up and down and I decided to send Lula and Chantelle on holiday to Marrakech for a week. I thought a break would give Chantelle time to process everything away from me rather than going through the stress of watching me suffer every day. While they were away my mum moved in with me and made sure I was ok, while I had a bit of me time, watching box sets on the sofa and a bit of football on the TV. Although my immediate family and friends were aware of the news, it was still a secret to the outside world. I'd spoken to Tranmere and they'd agreed not to release any information until I was ready for it to be put in the public domain.

When Chantelle and Lula returned from holiday, I decided it was time to break my silence. I drew up a statement with Lloydy, and Tranmere announced it on a Saturday morning. I remember being sat on my sofa at home when the news broke on Sky Sports News. The yellow breaking news strap flashed up on the screen and Jeff Stelling read my statement with a grimace. It was a surreal moment. Normally you're used to seeing your name up there if you've moved clubs or scored a goal, but now I was the topic of conversation for a very different reason. It was in those couple of minutes that it hit home that I was seriously ill. At first I was almost in denial, but when I saw it in front of me in black and white it almost served as confirmation. I sat there crying my eyes out, contemplating the worst-case scenario.

Within minutes my phone was going mental. I received text messages from current and former team-mates, as well as those I'd never even met before. On Twitter, I was overwhelmed with tweets of support from supporters and fellow cancer sufferers who assured me that I could win my fight. Reading through the messages raised my spirits and provided me with motivation. There was no use feeling sorry for myself, I had to stand up tall, puff my chest out and get ready for the biggest fight of my life.

Chapter 9
The fight

THERE was silence in the car as me and Chantelle sped down a lonely stretch of road. I rocked gently from side to side in the passenger seat and shut my eyes whilst taking long deep breaths to try and stave off the feeling of nausea, which was growing in my stomach. We continued for a few more minutes until I couldn't take it any longer.

'Stop the car!' I shouted. She slammed the brakes on and we came screeching to a halt. I flung the door open, stumbled out and threw up on the side of the road.

It was about 7pm on an early January evening in 2014. It was freezing cold outside and the sky was pitch black, but I was familiar with my surroundings. From the side of the road I could just about see the old pitches I used to train on at Carrington during my days at Manchester United. In the distance was the scene of so many happy memories from my childhood and teenage years, but here, on the other side of the fence, I was going through hell. I'd come full circle but in the worst possible fashion.

We were on our way home after I'd undergone a full day of chemotherapy treatment. The feeling afterwards isn't like car sickness or a hangover after a night on the booze. It's a very different experience and one that's so hard to describe properly, unless you've also had the misfortune of undergoing chemo. It's a spaced-out, sickening feeling, which is incomparable to anything else. This overwhelming sensation is often followed by violent retching, in my case at least, which leaves you bent double as your body ejects every last ounce of fluid from your system. At times the pain is excruciating.

I had the option of private treatment, which would've been paid for by Tranmere, but felt the NHS was the best option. Manchester's Christie Hospital is based in Withington, close to where I live, and is one of the largest cancer treatment centres in Europe. I was reassured by the prospect of being looked after by world-class experts who would give me the best possible chance of survival. My consultant would be Professor Radford, who had revealed the news of my diagnosis in November. He was the leading specialist in Hodgkin Lymphoma and blood cancers so I was delighted he'd be in charge of my case.

My team was assembled and ready for a six-month fight, but my team-mates on my ward were not as I'd expected. Despite the fact I was 23, had a partner and was the father of a little girl, I was told I'd be placed on the children's ward. I was shocked to see kids around me as young as four, who were closer to Lula in age than I was. The cut-off age for patients on the ward is 25, which meant I was the eldest there. I can't lie, I felt uncomfortable when I arrived and initially thought there must've been a mistake. I soon realised there hadn't when a couple of the kids came up to me having been told that a footballer would be joining them.

Before that moment, I used to think of cancer as a disease that just preyed on old people. I thought of the adverts you see on TV which showed people fighting the disease in their 70s and 80s. Suddenly, I realised how wrong I was. There were children with me who had pretty much only known cancer and hospital wards since they were born. What sort of childhood is that? In that moment, I decided that I had a role to play and a higher purpose to serve. I was the eldest and I would be the strong one on our ward. I needed to be a role model for them, by raising their spirits when they were down and showing them how they could fight and beat cancer.

I'll never forget one of the children I met, who was on a bed a few yards away from mine. She was a little girl, who couldn't have been any older than six. She had thick blonde hair like a Barbie doll, but large clumps had started to fall out, so she had long locks interspersed with large bald patches. It was so cruel and looked like something out of a horror film. She'd often climb off her bed and go and play on a small pool table in a little play area where the kids could escape and have a bit of fun when they weren't hooked up to machines or receiving injections. I decided to start joining her and would often rack the balls up in the triangle for her and try to make her laugh, but I don't think I ever saw her smile.

I can't tell you how hard that was to watch. She should've been outside playing with her friends at the park and enjoying life, but instead she was fighting cancer. As well as her physical battle, emotionally she had to deal with seeing her hair slowly falling out every time she looked in the mirror. She must've wondered why she didn't look like the other kids on TV and in the magazines on her bedside table. I watched on when her parents came to visit every day. I can't even imagine the pain they were going through and it made me feel for my own mum, who will always see me as her baby. I spoke to a counsellor about the anxiety I felt seeing her and the other kids suffering every day, but he reminded me to focus on my own journey.

My emotions were scrambled ahead of my first day of chemo. On one hand I was frightened of the unknown. I'd done so much research online but I knew I wouldn't have all the answers until I started my treatment. The same questions were still running through my head. What would it feel like? What would the side effects be? How would my body change as the treatment began to make its mark? I was also concerned how my illness would affect Chantelle and Lula. I knew it would put a strain on family life because I wouldn't be the same active father and partner I'd been up until that point. Equally, I was relieved to be starting chemo after weeks of waiting. At last we were going to start fighting back and slowing the tide of cancer flooding my body.

Each session of chemo normally lasted a full day, from 9am until about 7pm. I'd have a very light breakfast before I started because I knew I'd throw it back up later on. I'd also take anti-sickness tablets, but while they worked for some patients they did little to help me. The chemo itself is a cocktail of anti-cancer drugs designed to kill cancer cells. There are more than 100 different types of drugs used to fight different types of cancer. Doctors decide which ones to administer based on a range of factors, from where the cancer first appears in a patient's body, what the cells look like under a microscope, how advanced it is, where it has spread to, as well as your age and general health.

All the cells in your body grow by dividing in two. Some of them are designed to repair damage in the body, but when cancer attacks them it forces them to divide again and again until there is a mass of cells or a tumour. Chemo attacks these dividing cells but also some healthy cells, which multiply often, like hair or nail cells, which is why people lose their hair. Luckily, most healthy cells can recover after the treatment has finished, so while I knew in the short term my appearance might change, I was reassured that I would return to my normal physical self in the event everything went to plan and I emerged cancer free.

Before my first session began, I had to sit up in bed and wait while the chemo warmed up after being removed from a fridge. My nurse explained that it would be administered via a cannula, a thin tube inserted into my vein on my forearm. Some patients have a PICC line. This is another type of tube, which is put into a vein just above your elbow. The line is then thread along until it reaches a large vein in your chest. It remains there throughout the course of your treatment and is held in place by a dressing. Luckily I was spared the latter option because I had a large supply of healthy veins, which would transport the drugs around my body.

My heart started beating faster as I felt the chemo entering my veins. It was cold and I could feel it travelling up my arm and into my chest. The feeling was alien, like a foreign invasion slithering and spreading through my body. In my head I hated every second of it, but I smiled at the nurse and Chantelle, who was sat by the side of the bed, and said, 'this isn't so bad'. As usual, it was all bravado; I was just trying to put on a brave front so they thought I was ok. I certainly didn't want Chantelle to worry any more than she was doing already and also hoped that the other children on the ward might see me smiling and feel a bit less worried about their own treatment.

I settled in for a long day, but luckily I wasn't alone. I had various box sets and books to keep me entertained as the hours ticked away, but also the company of two other patients undergoing the same treatment. Nadia was a couple of years younger than me and we spoke to each other for hours about our lives, fears and what we were going to do once we'd both beaten cancer. We also told each other how we were feeling after each round of chemo, which I found to be therapeutic. She openly admitted she was from a privileged background, which again showed that even wealth is no defence against cancer. A guy called Carl was another of my comrades on the ward. He was always horrendously sick during the treatment, but I'd try to lighten the mood by giving him a bit of stick. 'Come on Carl, I'm only two hours in here, I can't handle another seven hours of this, mate,' I said through the curtain.

It's amazing how the support of a team of people can boost your morale. Having Nadia and Carl, as well as the rest of the children on the ward, with me on my journey created that sense of team spirit. We were all in the shit but we were in it together and determined that nobody was going to be left behind. My Twitter page became a constant source of support, with messages from fans, other cancer patients and survivors of the disease, all willing me on to win my battle. There are days when you're feeling a bit down and lost in your own thoughts, but when you see kind words from someone you've never even met it puts a smile on your face and sometimes brings a tear to your eye. The messages were like a tap, which helped to keep my emotional glass half full.

I was also astonished by the amount of people from within football who reached out to get in touch. Lloydy is the most well-connected person I know and he got hold of Bryan Robson to tell him about my situation. He'd beaten throat cancer in 2011, so although his experience was a bit different to mine, he understood what I was going through. I was blown away when I picked up the phone shortly after I started chemo and heard his voice on the other end of the line. It was surreal; I'd heard so many stories about Captain Marvel when I was at Manchester United and now he was giving me bits of advice and telling me to call him if I needed anything.

Stiliyan Petrov was another high-profile figure that took the time to speak to me at length about his battle with cancer. In 2012 he was diagnosed with leukaemia and was 12 months into what turned out to be a four-year battle with the disease when he called me for a chat. The treatment had really affected him mentally. He hadn't been able to see his children for long periods because his immune system was so weak. The risk of infection from one of his kids was too great and could've killed him, so he'd only seen them two or three times in 12 months. My situation was bad but his struggle did put things into perspective, at least. I was in a position where I was in hospital every couple of weeks, whereas he was practically living there.

There was another person who gave me real hope of not only surviving cancer but also making a return to football. Ross Hutchins was a tennis doubles player but we had so much in common. Like me, he was in peak physical condition when he was diagnosed with Hodgkin Lymphoma, aged 28, in 2012. He'd initially complained of backache, which gradually grew worse. At one point it was that bad he was only getting an hour's sleep and tried and failed to relieve the pain by lying on top of tennis balls on his bathroom floor to try and massage his back. Eventually he started to experience many of the same symptoms I had. The glands on his neck were swollen and he was always tired, but after seeing six different physiotherapists, they still didn't know what was wrong with him.

He underwent tests, which his doctors thought would reveal a kidney problem, only for them to find out he was actually suffering from cancer. Even worse, it had spread to his lungs, spleen and back. At the time, Ross and his doubles partner, Colin Fleming, were ranked in the world's top ten and it seemed impossible that he would be able to recover and then get back on the carousel of professional tennis. But Ross is as stubborn as they come, and when he called me he'd just played in his first tournament since being given the all-clear, and had also come through a gruelling pre-season training camp in Miami with his close friend Andy Murray.

I was inspired by his comeback and his incredible mindset. Somehow, he'd remained positive throughout and had even continued to work on different projects outside tennis during his treatment. He couldn't play while he was undergoing chemo, but he'd refused to let his illness put the rest of his life on hold. I continued to text him frequently, to the point where he was probably sick of me pestering him, though he never once complained. He was playing in different tournaments all over the world, so I knew that he'd probably be in bed sometimes when I texted him, but he would always get back to me with bits of advice, from dealing with chemo, to his fitness regime and diet during his recovery.

I found it frustrating spending long periods in bed. I was used to training five days a week and the competitive release of matches. Hard exercise is a bit of a drug; it gives you a high and makes you feel good about yourself, but without it I found my mood became quite down. My mind was exhausted from overthinking, but my body still felt capable of doing some light work. In the two weeks between every chemo session I tried to do core exercises to stop my physique from withering away, but afterwards I felt terrible. My stomach was already sore from all the retching, which made it difficult to hold certain positions.

The routine of chemo was always the same. After a full day at the hospital, Chantelle would pick me up, take me home and then put me into bed. For the following four days I'd feel horrendous and spend most of my time in bed before I gradually started to turn the corner. I had time to kill between my visits to the hospital, so I decided to use it effectively by exploring alternative therapies. My Tranmere team-mate James Rowe told me about his dad's battle with throat cancer and explained how he'd been to see a lady called Kimberly who had helped him to optimise his rest so that he recovered as efficiently as possible between bouts of chemo. I was a bit sceptical at first, but I did some research online and thought it was worth a go. When your life is in danger you'll try anything to boost your chances of survival.

Kimberly lived in Newbury, which was a four-hour drive from Manchester, but Chantelle took me there every weekend for six months. James's parents let her and Lula stay with them, while I lived with Kimberly for two days and focused on my rest. Her expertise focused on a Japanese form of relaxation therapy called reiki. The aim was to make sure my chakras were in alignment, which are various centres of energy within the body, which are said to regulate human processes, from organ function to emotional wellbeing. Her sessions eased my anxiety and I always slept deeply while I was there, which gave me a physical and mental boost.

My sixth session of chemo marked the halfway stage of my treatment. I felt like I was at the top of the hill and the home straight was in sight. My mum, Reuben and his girlfriend, Sarah, joined Chantelle at the hospital, but I was feeling rough so they went to the canteen for a bit. While they were there I could see a girl walking down the ward. As she came closer I realised it was my ex-girlfriend, Lucy. I thought the chemo must've been giving me hallucinations. What on earth was she doing here? I was looking and feeling terrible so it was the worst possible time to see her.

She'd spoken to me over the phone when the news had broken about my diagnosis, but I could tell she was still shocked to see me lying there. She tried to cover it up by telling me that I looked well. 'Liar!' I replied with a laugh. She explained that she was visiting her mum, Christine, who had been suffering from cancer for quite some time and had bumped into Chantelle in the canteen. She stayed for about 25 minutes and later on I saw her dad, Dave, while I was going to the toilet with my sick bowl. He said he was doing fine but admitted he was finding it hard seeing his wife in so much pain. I had to bring an abrupt end to our chance encounter to be sick in the toilet, but I was happy our paths had crossed.

Although I was still being violently sick, I was fortunate that physically I hadn't altered drastically in appearance. My face was puffy, I'd lost a bit of weight and started to lose my hair, but I still felt that I looked like me. I've always taken pride in my appearance so that came as a big relief. However, there was still no way of knowing whether or not I was winning my war with cancer. I underwent various tests to monitor my white and red blood cell count, which provided an indicator of my general health, but I would only know for certain if it had done the business at the end of the six months, when I'd have a series of scans. It was hard thinking that all of the pain and suffering might have been for nothing, but I told myself that if I was feeling that bad it must mean it was nailing the cancer. I was also confident that if I could get through this then I'd be strong enough to fight anything else in the future.

It was 5 May when I had my final dose of chemo. I felt like a boxer at the end of a gruelling training camp. I was relieved it was all over but nervous about what would happen next. There was a two-week wait between my last day at hospital and the date I was given to return for my results. I was delighted it was all over, but I was also sad to leave behind some of the friends I'd made on the ward. I wanted to believe that everyone in there would make a full recovery but I knew that not all of those children would make it out. I sometimes wonder what happened to the girl with the Barbie blonde hair and hope and pray that she's got a full head of hair again and is playing with her friends in the playground.

A sense of déjà vu came over me as Chantelle drove me to get my results. The last time we made this journey our world had been torn apart. If it was bad news, I knew the prognosis was bleak. My cancer was advanced and if six months of chemo hadn't shifted it then it was unlikely another treatment would be able to do the job. We walked into Professor Radford's office and sat down on two seats in front of his desk. My heart felt it was beating out of my chest. I had friends and family at home waiting to find out the news and I couldn't bear the thought of telling them the chemo hadn't been a success. I felt like he was speaking in slow motion as he started to explain the results of my scans. I was on the edge of my seat, hanging on every word that came out of his mouth.

'I'm very pleased to say that you're now cancer free, Joe,' he said. A feeling of relief and elation surged through my veins. I grabbed Chantelle and hugged her as tightly as I could. I felt like jumping up and down and swinging off the light fitting on the ceiling. I'd never felt so happy in my entire life and couldn't wipe the smile off my face. The chemo had worked as well as could've been expected and the only thing that had been left behind was some scar tissue, which I was reassured would disappear pretty quickly. 'So when can I start playing football again?' I asked him and my nurse, Rachael Campsey, who had been there throughout my treatment. 'I thought you might ask me that,' said Professor Radford. 'You need to take some time out to rest. Your body has gone through extreme stress and it needs to recover. You could play again but it's going to take time for you to get back to where you were before.'

I had the answer I needed. Before we left the office, I asked one of the staff to take a picture of the four of us. I was so grateful for their help and all the nurses at Christie Hospital for saving my life. We jumped in the car and drove home, but this time laughter filled the air and the feeling that we were about to embark on a fresh start. The future was ours again.

I'd listened to Professor Radford's advice, but I also knew that football doesn't wait for anyone and I knew I'd be forgotten about if I didn't return as quickly as possible. I was out of contract and didn't know what would happen next, but there were six weeks before players would return for pre-season which would give me the perfect opportunity to work on my fitness while everyone else was lying on the beach. Just hours after being given the all-clear, I had started to plot my comeback.

Chapter 10

P45

THE letterbox slammed shut and an envelope landed on the hallway floor with a thud. I dragged myself off the sofa with a groan and trudged through to pick up the morning mail. As I bent down, I could see the Tranmere Rovers crest stamped on the front and tore open the seal like a child opening their Christmas presents.

Two weeks had passed since I'd been given the all-clear and now I was waiting for news of a different kind. The two-year deal I'd signed upon joining the club had come to an end and I was now out of contract. For nine months I'd been no use to them, but I thought I'd be offered a short-term deal on reduced terms so I could prove my fitness, but so far I'd heard nothing and was beginning to fear the worst.

I unfolded the envelope and quickly scanned the letter to see what had been put on the table, and mouthed the words written in black ink as I read them. 'Dear Joe Thompson, thanks for all your hard work for Tranmere Rovers Football

1989. Me enjoying a snooze with mum when I was just a few months old.

1993. My face sums up my mood around the time Reuben was born.

2001. (Top left) Grinning like a Cheshire cat after joining Manchester United. Tom Cleverley (bottom, second from right) was the one that made it to the first team, but a lot of these boys went on to forge careers elsewhere.

2006. Getting stuck in on my full debut away at MK Dons.

2007. I won the League Two Apprentice of the Year prize at the end of my first season. It's still one of my proudest achievements.

January 2009. Three is the magic number. My confidence was through the roof after I scored a hat-trick in the opening 17 minutes against Aldershot aged 19.

2012. Running down the wing in my first season at Tranmere Rovers. I started well but had a disappointing campaign.

2013. The Fresh Prince of Prenton Park. I'd do anything to have that trim again!

2013. My Tranmere team-mates, fans and a host of other players grew their hair for a charity I set up called #grow4joe during my first battle with cancer.

Me and Lula shortly after she was born. I feared I was too young to be a dad but all my worries melted away the moment I first saw her.

2013. All the Tranmere lads showing their support by wearing Thompson No. 7 shirts. My face had become really puffy following chemotherapy.

2014. Smiling from ear to ear with Lula, my nurse Rachel Campsey and Professor Radford after being told I'm in remission and cancer free.

2015. Celebrating with my team-mate and housemate, Charlie Wyke, at Carlisle. My time at Brunton Park was one of the happiest 12 months of my career.

Me and Chantelle tying the knot in front of family and friends in Ibiza. The entire day was perfect from start to finish.

Enjoying the moment. We've come a long way since our first date at the cinema.

Reuben, me and Chantelle's dad, Paul. We brought the wedding forward a year to make sure he was well enough to make it. I'm so happy he got to walk his girl down the aisle.

Me and Lloydy on my wedding day. He was the closest thing to a father figure that I've had in my life.

(Left to right) The boys looking well. My groomsmen, Nicky Blackman and James Rothwell and best man, Reuben, before I said my vows.

2017. Me and Lula attending my final Rochdale game before I started chemotherapy treatment after being diagnosed with cancer for the second time.

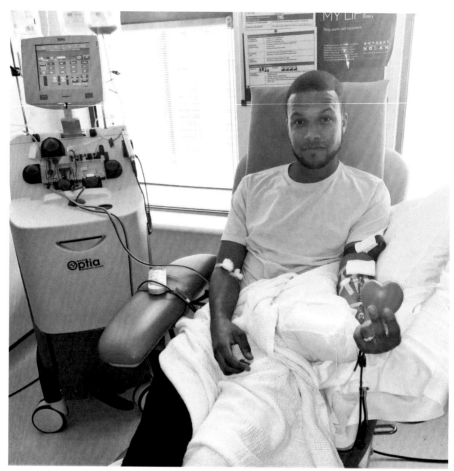

2017. Midway through my treatment my remaining healthy cells were harvested ahead of my stem cell transplant.

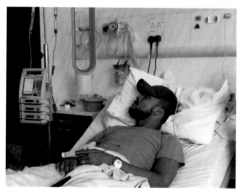

2017. Literally living off machines. Needing blood transfusions to try and raise my red and white blood cell count. They were some of the longest days of my life. Torture!

2017. I defied doctor's orders and told Chantelle to bring Lula into my isolation room for a brief visit on Father's Day. She was my shining light on what was my darkest day.

2017. After 18 days in isolation, I hobbled out of hospital with Lula and Chantelle weighing just 10 stone.

2017. All smiles after Dr Gibbs gave me the all-clear. The relief I felt that day is impossible to describe.

2017. Me giving my first motivational talk to Sheffield Wednesday's under-23 squad at Cassius Camps just a few weeks after finishing my treatment.

2017. Laughing and joking with Keith Hill and some of my Rochdale team-mates on my first day back at training.

2018. From the ward to Wembley. It was a dream come true running on to the pitch as a second half substitute in Rochdale's 6-1 defeat to Tottenham in our FA Cup fifth round replay, eight months after getting the all-clear.

What a feeling. My second half goal gave Rochdale a 1-0 win over Charlton and saved us from relegation on the final day of the season. That moment was written in the stars. My family were all so proud of me! What a whirlwind year.

Me and my two beautiful girls at the christening of our friends' little boy, Hendrix. After everything we've been through we're stronger than ever before. Teamwork!

Club, but we won't be retaining your services beyond this season. Good luck for the future.'

My heart sank. I sat and stared at the letter for a moment and then threw it across the room. I was so angry. I couldn't believe they had cut me loose after everything I'd been through, and they didn't even have the decency to call me. The supporters had been incredible. I'd had messages from hundreds of them asking me when I was going to be back and telling me they couldn't wait to see me wearing the number seven shirt again next season. Now I knew I'd never wear it again.

A lot had changed at Tranmere whilst I'd been undergoing chemotherapy. The club had sacked Ronnie Moore in April 2014 after the FA had found him guilty of breaching betting rules and a month later they were relegated to League Two. A host of players had been released in a bid to balance the books, and given that I was earning good money they'd decided to cut their losses. From a financial and playing point of view, I was now seen as a risk because they didn't know if I'd ever return to my previous level.

I felt rejected, just as I had done when Manchester United had released me as a 15-year-old. Back then I'd realised just how ruthless football was and now I'd been given another reminder. It doesn't matter who you are or what you've been through, clubs are businesses and there is little place for empathy. If you're seen as a drain on resources, particularly lower down the leagues, then you'll get the boot and join the hundreds of other players desperately hunting for a new club during the summer months.

Chantelle was sat next to me and had read the letter. I looked at her face and could tell she was shocked. 'Shit, the fucking bastards,' she said. 'Joe, where are we going to get the money from?' It was a good question but I didn't have an answer. During my treatment we'd cut down on all our outgoings and got rid of anything that we could do without so we could save money. We were running around in a little Vauxhall Corsa and a Renault Clio. We had to be financially strict in case I was told I'd never play again. We had a little pot of money together but it wasn't going to last us very long with a mortgage to pay and a little girl to feed.

I picked up the phone and called Lloydy to tell him the news. 'Gaz, we're fucked mate,' I said. 'I know we are mate, but don't worry, I'll make a few calls and see what I can do,' he replied. I was only 23 but it's hard enough getting a new club if you've had a serious injury, never mind cancer. I had a good set of GCSEs behind me and a BTEC sports diploma, but that wasn't going to be enough to get me a decent job if I didn't play football again. I began to think I'd end up stacking shelves at a supermarket and we'd have to sell our house to make ends meet if I didn't pull my finger out.

I started to do the sums in my head. I knew that I had my final pay packet in the bank and would receive some severance pay, which would buy me a bit of time, but realistically I had six to eight weeks to get something sorted or I'd be in the shit financially. The PFA had been a huge help while I'd been out and had added another couple of hundred pounds to my pay packet every month to help pay for the cost of additional childcare when Chantelle was at work or visiting me in hospital. I knew I'd have to speak to them again for advice. I didn't have any critical illness insurance, so I wouldn't get a payout if I was forced to retire. Chantelle had also reduced the number of clients on her books because she needed to be at home looking after me, so she couldn't support both of us on her wage alone.

I'd been in a privileged position financially and was probably earning more money than most people my age, but I wasn't being paid hundreds of thousands of pounds a week. I was on £1,200 a week, plus healthy bonuses if I was playing, which I obviously hadn't been. It was a lot for someone my age, but at the same time I'd only been on good money for a few years. During that time I'd bought a car and saved up a deposit for a house, and had to provide for my first child. Although we'd been living comfortably, I didn't have ten years of earnings behind me on Premier League money. I now get why players lower down the leagues move for financial reasons because a footballer's career is a short one and you don't have the same opportunity to restock the pot once you're retired. Someone in a normal job will be earning until they're 60 or 65, whereas a player will often have to retrain for another career because he has no qualifications or experience to fall back on.

Today's players also don't have access to their football pension until they're 65. Luckily, I was in the last age group who could immediately tap into their pension at 35, but I'd only been a professional for five years, so I knew I wouldn't have a huge sum of money to fall back on. Hindsight is a wonderful thing, but looking back I wish I'd stashed some more money away for a rainy day or even invested in myself and studied for other qualifications away from the pitch. I tell young players to do that now, rather than wasting their money on pointless things like clothes and expensive trainers. Ollie Rathbone is my little project at Rochdale, he's a good player and very smart and is always asking how he should invest his money. I wish there were more young lads with their heads screwed on like him, but being financially savvy and learning new skills is easier said than done when you're already trying to learn a trade and work your way up the football ladder. There was no point in me thinking what I could or should have done; these were the cards I'd been dealt and I had to get on with it.

The first thing I had to do was get fit. Professor Radford had told me to rest but I couldn't just sit on a sofa for weeks and then turn up for a trial and expect to win a contract. I hadn't kicked a ball for nine months and decided to start rebuilding my fitness with road running. Several nights a week I'd put Lula to bed, then pull on my running trainers and put my earphones in before setting off around the roads of Prestwich. They were lonely nights, pounding the pavements and mulling over my worries in my head. In a way, it felt like I was a kid again, running cross country and pretending I was Rocky, except now the only competition I had was myself. I had no fitness plan or regime. At first, I just ran from lamppost to lamppost, to see how I felt and how hard I could push myself. The following night I'd add another five minutes on or sprint a bit harder between lampposts so I knew I was improving.

When I looked at myself in the mirror, my body didn't look much different to how it had done nine months ago, but I could feel the difference the morning after each run. My hamstrings, calves and feet were in agony. I realised my legs were basically hollow. There was enough strength in them to get me around my route, but none of the endurance I knew I'd need to sprint repeatedly up and down a football pitch. The minute I put my foot down and tried to run a little faster for a prolonged period, I felt like my tank suddenly ran out of gas. That was a worry, but I tried to keep any negative thoughts out of my head and told myself that everything would return to normal in time.

Every day I called Lloydy in the hope of good news, but each time the message was the same: 'I've got nothing yet, Joe, he likes the look of you as a player but doesn't want to take a risk, but don't worry, we'll sort something out.' It was a pattern that continued for another month until an old mate came to the rescue. Dave Flitcroft had been given the manager's job at Bury after leaving Barnsley following the sacking of Keith Hill. We'd always got along really well and he'd called Lloydy and asked him if he thought I could get back to my best. His reply was a firm 'yes' and so Flickers invited me in to do some tests. I was dreading it. He was obsessed with fitness so I knew the other players would be in great shape. I'd worked hard for the previous month but that was no preparation for the sort of beasting I was likely to get.

The first test I had to do was called a VO2 max, which pushes your mind and body to the limit. It measures your maximal consumption of oxygen and the efficiency of your muscles during exercise of increasing intensity. I had to put on a mask and run on a treadmill for as long as possible as the pace got faster and faster. With this test, there is no hiding place, because your heart rate is on a screen so the staff know how hard you're working and how much you've got left in the tank. I worked my bollocks off and put my heart and soul into every stride, and when I finished the run there was literally nothing left in my legs. I was wearing a harness, which whipped me off the machine. Afterwards, I laid on the floor dripping in sweat and gasping for breath.

Remarkably I'd done better than a lot of the other players and my performance prompted Flickers to invite me in for pre-season training. I was one step closer to a contract, but I knew more hard work was to follow. I think I speak for most footballers when I say the beep test is the one we all dread every summer. I felt sick as we lined up ready to start, much like I'd done when I used to wait for the gun to sound at my athletics races. I told myself I wouldn't be the first to drop out. If you're that guy then your reputation is in tatters and you simply haven't worked hard enough during the summer. The player who drops out second is almost as bad. He's a coward in my eyes because he's seen that someone else has also quit and thinks he can do so without suffering the embarrassment of the first player. That's just my opinion, but he's probably got plenty more in the tank and is happy to sit on the side and watch the rest of his team-mates suffer. Providing I wasn't either of those two, I thought I'd have done myself justice, but I exceeded my own expectations by finishing in the middle of the pack, even ahead of some of the youngest and supposedly fittest players in the squad.

My efforts exposed a few of the younger lads, including an 18-year-old called Regan Walker, who Flickers called out in front of the whole team. 'He's had chemotherapy for six months, how has he beaten you?' he shouted at him. Regan admitted to me later on that he hadn't put the work in during the summer and had been found out. He was released soon after and played non-league football for a while, but later that year he was diagnosed with bone cancer in his femur.

It turned out he'd been suffering with horrific pain in one of his legs for months. At one point it was that bad he passed out but continued playing in the belief it would pass. I was stunned. I knew how he was feeling. Luckily, after 12 months of chemotherapy, he made a full recovery, but cancer ended his career at the age of 21 after parts of his leg had to be removed along with the tumour. I still keep in contact with him and he knows I'm only ever a phone call away if he needs my help.

That day had been a wake-up call for Regan, but for me it was the moment I realised I wasn't finished. Physically, I was still some way off being 100 per cent fit, but I knew I could compete and that did wonders for my confidence. It also convinced the club to offer me a 12-month deal on £600 a week. It was a big drop in pay, but it was better than being on the dole and gave me breathing space and an opportunity to work on my fitness for a year. The squad was aiming for promotion, and I thought if I could hang on to the coat-tails of the other players and make a few appearances then in a year's time I'd be in a good position to play regularly in League One and Two.

After a brutal first few days of pre-season training, we headed to Tenerife to continue our preparations for the new season. I got through the sessions but realised that my recovery was a lot slower than it had been before. I had to work on my body like a Formula One car to make sure I was ready to train again each day. I was having ice baths, switching between hot and cold showers, using foam rollers and having massages to ease the pain in my legs. When the masseur, Nick Meace, first got to work on me, he was alarmed at the lumps he could feel in my quads. 'Fucking hell, what the hell is inside these?' He asked me. My lymphatic system still wasn't flushing properly, so my legs were clogged up with fluid and lactic acid. My back and joints were killing me as well, because I'd lost muscle mass after spending days at a time lying in bed.

Flickers had been watching me from afar and wanted to know what my goals were for the next six months. I didn't expect to feature that much, and my first target was just to be on the bench and be ready to make an impact. I didn't want to be in the squad for the sake of it if I knew I wasn't capable of performing. Beyond that, I wanted to get a goal because I knew it would give me a massive confidence boost. Regardless of my illness, there was pressure on me to return. Flickers had taken a risk by offering me a contract and he wanted a return on his investment. Bury had a good budget that year, but he couldn't afford to carry dead wood, especially when this was his first managerial position. He'd done me a favour and I had no intention of letting him down, but, for all my efforts in pre-season, the road back to professional football was tougher than I thought.

Away from the pitch, Chantelle and I had learnt from our financial mistakes. We'd been saving as much money as possible and spotted an opportunity to invest in our future. A salon had become available near our house, but the owner was asking for £30,000. We didn't have the cash, but decided to keep tabs on it and see if we could strike a deal further down the line. She's incredibly driven and already had a long list of clients, including the wives and girlfriends of a few footballers, many of whom were based in suburban Manchester, so we knew there was the potential for her to start her own business, which would provide us with another source of income.

Six months later, the salon was still available and we decided to barter with the owner. We'd been saving every penny we had and proposed a down payment of £10,000 and then additional money over a period of time. He accepted the offer, but now we had to work out how to actually run a salon. We got the keys but didn't even know how the till worked or who did the water and electric. One thing we did know was that it would take time before we turned a profit. Chantelle would have to invest in hiring staff, buying products and also advertise the business in the local area and hope she could attract enough clients to at least break even. It was a risk, but she has a sound business head on her and an incredible work ethic. If anyone was going to make a success of the place, it was her.

Back at Bury, my progress had been stop-start, and Flickers was growing frustrated. I was fit but I kept on picking up little niggles and knocks which would set me back a few weeks. I came on against Hemel Hempstead in the FA Cup and changed the game, but my performance almost hindered me. He expected me to be able to repeat my performances every week and I just couldn't do it. On some occasions I just wasn't fit enough to play, and when I did it could then take me a week to recover and I wouldn't be ready for the next match. My touch and anticipation, which comes with playing regular games, was also below par, so I couldn't express myself as I wanted to. He didn't understand that I still probably shouldn't have been anywhere near a football pitch and that I was already over-extending myself.

He decided to loan me out to Wrexham, who were in the Conference, so I could play regular games at a lower level and hopefully get my confidence back. I felt like I was under so much pressure and my enjoyment for the game went out of the window. If I couldn't impress at that level, what hope did I have of doing so in the Football League every week? I hated everything about Conference football, even down to the footballs, which were hard and plastic and made by a brand called Jako. I'd played with Mitre balls since I was a kid and I had to relearn how to control and bend the ball because it felt completely different. The pitches were heavy and the games were 100mph. There didn't seem to be any pattern to the play. In the Football League, the midfielder wins the second ball and then feeds the wide players. It's then my job to beat the full-back and whip the ball in. The Conference was like pinball and the game would pass me by for large periods because defenders would just lump it up the pitch.

A hamstring injury meant I wasn't there long, but as soon as I recovered I was loaned out to Southport. Their manager, Paul Carden, called me and told me he wanted me to do him a favour and help to keep them up. In return, he said I'd play every week and get my fitness up. It seemed like a fair deal, but again I didn't cover myself in glory. I felt like I was clinging on by the skin of my teeth. I was on the fringes of games and had to push myself to my absolute maximum just to compete. I just couldn't play at the same intensity anymore. Inwardly, I thought I was finished. My body had gone. My athleticism had been one of my strongest qualities, but you can't play as a winger if your pace and endurance have vanished. I returned to Bury for the rest of the season and knew I couldn't be loaned out again because I'd now played for three clubs in one season. One more would've been a breach of Football League rules.

When I returned, my head was gone and I wasn't enjoying being there. My mood wasn't helped by the fact I'd never seen eye to eye with Flickers' assistant, Ben Futcher. We'd come up against each other many times on the pitch and I'd always given him plenty of stick for being a slow, burly centre-back. But in the end it wasn't him that I ended up falling out with. Flickers had always been a bit of a mentor, but I felt that he'd changed since becoming a manager. I struggled to deal with criticism from him because Keith had always been the boss at Rochdale, whereas he was the one who'd put an arm around your shoulder. I had huge respect for him as a man for helping me out when others wouldn't touch me with a bargepole, but our relationship was never the same again after we had a furious argument.

The tension between us had been simmering for weeks when he pulled me into a suite at Bury's ground. 'I'm not sure you're going to get back to where you were before,' he said. I was stunned. 'You're my manager, you're the one who is meant to believe in me,' I replied. He still had more to get off his chest. 'What I'm seeing just isn't good enough, you're letting your family down Joe,' he continued. There was a moment of silence. He'd pressed the red button. 'Do you want me to tell you how it fucking is?' I shouted. 'Go on then, get it off your chest,' he said. 'I've won the biggest fight I'll ever have,' I said. 'I was fighting for them when I was in hospital, so don't you fucking tell me that I've let them down.' Our row continued until we were interrupted by one of my team-mates, Nicky Adams, who put his head around the door and then quickly retreated. Minutes later the chairman did the same thing, but thought better of trying to intervene.

Flickers told me how tough it had been for him telling his wife and kids he'd been sacked by Barnsley, but he didn't seem to understand that his problems were nothing like what I'd been through. On a professional level, I'm sure he was devastated to get sacked, but I know he would've been on good money and probably received a healthy pay-off upon receiving his P45. Management had changed him. You see it happen with a lot of ex-players when they move into coaching. I'd hoped that he would remember what it was like being a player, but it seemed like he just couldn't get his head around the fact it was going to take me longer than I thought to get back to my best. We continued to trade verbal blows until I stormed out, fetched my kitbag from the dressing room and drove home.

I knew then that I'd never play for Bury again. In training he tried to punish me for our argument by making me do ridiculous sessions in the gym. One of them involved me lifting weights that were far too heavy for me before doing a lap of the Gigg Lane pitch, alongside our second-choice goalkeeper, Shwan Jalal, who he also wanted to get rid of. I had to repeat it four or five times. He was taking the piss out of me, but I refused to let him break me.

On another occasion he made me do a circuit he called 'Ultrafit'. It had nothing to do with football fitness, it was just designed to break me mentally. I had to run uphill, do weights, Olympic lifts and then finish off on a machine called the grappler. I was in bits but I bit my tongue and didn't give him the reaction he craved. Instead, I questioned the coaches and asked them why they were insisting upon me doing the sessions when they knew full well what the situation was. They told me they were just carrying out orders. I felt sorry for them, particularly Jon Lucas, who I'd worked with at Rochdale and knew was a good guy. I knew they were all good at their jobs but if they defied the boss they could be out of work themselves.

I spent the final weeks of the season training with the youth team and playing crossbar challenge with the rest of the bomb squad – a term footballers use for fringe players who can't get a sniff of the first team. I watched on as the first team clinched promotion, ironically against Tranmere. Despite my situation, I genuinely wanted the lads to do well because I knew how hard they'd worked all season. To celebrate, the club paid for the whole squad and coaching staff to go on holiday to Marbella. The lads asked me if I wanted to join them and I decided I would. I knew I'd be leaving Bury at the end of the season and it would be the perfect way to say goodbye to everyone in the sun.

Unsurprisingly, Flickers wasn't happy. 'You shouldn't be here,' he said during our first night out over there. 'I tell you what, you stay out of my way and I'll stay out of yours,' I replied. He looked at me for a moment and then walked off. I went in the opposite direction and that was pretty much the last I saw of him for the remainder of the trip. He still messages me from time to time, but our relationship has never been the same since. Our personalities are very similar and in hindsight that's probably why we ended up clashing.

When we got back to Manchester Airport, I said goodbye to all the players and thanked them for pushing me over the past year. I'd enjoyed being a Shaker, even though my stay was only a brief one. Things hadn't worked out, but the players and supporters had always been supportive, which meant a lot. I jumped in a taxi and headed home knowing that I was back to square one, but I was in a far better position than I'd been a year ago. I had a full season of training under my belt and, although I hadn't played anywhere near as much or as well as I'd hoped, inwardly I retained the belief that eventually I'd be the player I once was. But to do that, I needed someone else to take a chance on me. I got home, put the kettle on and waited for the phone to ring.

Chapter 11
Survival of the fittest

IT must have been a peculiar sight for the staff at Manchester's JJB Soccerdome to see a couple of professional footballers meet up for a casual game of five-a-side. The season was over, but the sun was out, which meant it was time for me and the boys to have our annual summer fixture. Danny Simpson had gathered a group of lads on one of the pitches a couple of miles away from Old Trafford, where the two teams exchanged pre-match verbals and limbered up for battle.

It felt cathartic to play purely for fun in a game where there was no pressure to retain a starting place or satisfy thousands of fans who had paid to watch us play. It took me back to a simpler time when I used to kick a ball around the school playground or the local park. Back then I did it for the sheer enjoyment of playing and to escape to a happy place where I could forget about all my problems at home. When football is your job, and I know I'm lucky to call it that, at times you can lose the fun factor and forget why you fell in love with the game. I know I'm not the only player who feels the same way. In previous years Danny Welbeck, Micah Richards and Nicky Blackman have also joined in our small-sided games. Deep down, we all secretly loved being kids again.

There were no points at stake or fans watching on, except for a few bemused onlookers who had gathered to double check that there were indeed two professional footballers in a cage having a kickabout, but the game was still fiercely contested. Danny has been in the headlines a few times for the wrong reasons over the years and you might think he's a bit of a playboy, but he is without doubt the most competitive player I know. He'll happily smash you into the fence or put you over the hoardings, because he desperately wants to win at everything. If you're dribbling towards him he'll goad you to put you off your game. 'Come on then, come on then, run at me!' he shouted at me on this particular afternoon. 'It's five-a-side mate, why do you care so much?' I laughed.

Although he was never a regular at Manchester United, it's no surprise to me that he made a few first-team appearances and was accepted inside a dressing room run by Roy Keane because he has the same animalistic drive to win. It's a trait that's within all players to a certain extent; we're testosterone-fuelled beings who never grow out of that childlike hatred of losing. It's also probably one of the factors that separates those who make it and those who don't. If you're not emotionally invested in the outcome of a game then you can never match the intensity of a team-mate who is willing to do anything and everything to avoid the humiliation of failure. Talent will get you so far, but it'll never be fulfilled without that inner fire.

I know that flame burns inside me and that's exactly why I was playing five-a-side on that summer's afternoon. Six weeks after being released by Bury, I was still without a club and knew that I needed to stay fit so that I was ready if another team came calling. I also needed a competitive release after spending over a month kicking my heels. There's nothing better for your fitness than playing five-a-side and my legs were battered when I got home that afternoon. I started to run a hot bath because I knew they were going to be stiff the following day. Chantelle came into the bathroom and asked me if Lloydy had heard of any interest. I told her I still had no news, but just as the words left my lips, my phone started to ring in my pocket.

'Hello mate, how are you doing?' asked the voice on the end of the line. It was Keith Curle. 'Can you get up here tomorrow? I want to take a look at you.' I quickly tried to recall where he was managing and thankfully remembered he was at Carlisle United. 'Can I not come up on Wednesday?' I replied. I could tell that I was on loudspeaker and the rest of his coaching staff were listening in the background. 'Do you want to earn a fucking contract or not?' he laughed. I could've done with another 24 hours to make sure my legs were fresh but I had no choice. He told me to meet him at their training ground at 10am the following day. I put the postcode into my phone. Fuck. It was a two-hour drive. I hate driving long distances before playing football because you're never quite as sharp mentally. I decided I'd get up at 6am, stop off at a service station for a bit of breakfast and get there nice and early to make a good impression. But before that, I jumped in the bath for a hot soak, closed my eyes and prayed that my legs recovered in time.

The following morning my alarm went off and I was relieved to find that my legs were in good working order. After a brief pit stop for some pre-training fuel, I arrived at the car park at 8am, where Keith was stood waiting for me. Before we'd even shaken hands we both burst out laughing. We were wearing the exact same outfit; shorts, trainers and a casual shirt. I was impressed with his physical appearance. He was 50 but still looked like he could pull on a pair of boots and do a job if needed. He was lean and healthy and his calves were the size of shot puts. If I look like him at the same age, I'll be very happy. On the drive up, I'd remembered watching him as a player. He was a tough left-back for Manchester City, Wolves, Sheffield United and a few other clubs, but there was nothing old school about his management style. He was forward thinking, and, though his will to win was still as strong as ever, he didn't rant and rave at his players unless he had to. Instead, he preferred to deliver his bollockings in small doses when you least expected it.

As I got changed into my tracksuit, I felt like I was backstage preparing for an audition. It turned out I was one of 12 trialists, so there was no guarantee I was going to win a contract. I eyed up the competition and didn't recognise any of the faces, which I felt gave me an advantage. I'd played against a lot of the Carlisle lads, so they already knew what I was about, while my old Rochdale team-mate Jason Kennedy played for them, so I instantly had a connection in the dressing room. I was impressed with the facilities; they had two training grounds, while their Brunton Park stadium could hold nearly 18,000 people. It wasn't a million miles away from Manchester, either, so I could already see myself playing for them. The training was intense but perfectly tailored to the demands of a game. The club had a brilliant fitness coach, Lee Fearn, who communicated very clearly exactly how long each part of the session needed to be and how hard we needed to work. We all had to wear GPS monitors so he could measure the physical output of every individual and tailor training accordingly.

After the first day, Keith came up to me and told me he wanted me to stay there for the rest of the week. I rang Chantelle up and said I wouldn't be coming home until the weekend, so she'd need to sort out childcare while I was away. She was encouraged by the news and told me to give it my all, even though she would now have to be a single mum for the next few days. These are some of the sacrifices that wives and girlfriends of footballers have to make that people don't see. We couldn't afford the luxury of employing a nanny, and would never wish to either, so she had to juggle the running of our home and her business, while worrying whether I'd have a new job at the end of the week.

As each day passed, Keith and his staff crossed another name or two off their shortlist of trialists. I was relieved to be one of four remaining players who made the cut for the Thursday morning session. He'd seen our skills up close and how we'd adapted to his style of training and the Carlisle dressing room. But that still wasn't enough. His recruitment process was meticulous and he wanted to learn a bit more about our characters. He told us all not to over-exert ourselves in the afternoon because we would need to meet at the training ground at 6am on Friday morning. We were all going on a road trip, but the destination was kept a secret. The lads who had worked under Keith the previous season didn't even know where we were going. This was going to be no holiday camp, we were heading to a boot camp.

The morning sun had risen from its slumber as a weary squad of players wiped the sleep from their eyes and climbed aboard a white minibus parked up at the training ground. For the next hour we rattled down an endless series of country lanes towards our mystery destination. The further we travelled, the further we appeared to be from civilisation. As I looked out of the window, all I could see for miles was green grass, sheep and a beautiful blue sky. We eventually came to a narrow, winding road, leading to a vast country estate, which looked like something out of a period drama. We'd arrived at Graythwaite Hall, a privately-run family estate perched on the shores of Lake Windermere. It's the most tranquil of settings, where people can come on holiday and rent out various cottages on the site, but that wasn't why we were there.

The estate has another identity. It's also the home of Cassius Camps, a punishing boot camp where professional football and rugby clubs send their players to test their physical and mental mettle during pre-season. As we climbed out of the minibus and stretched our legs, three black Range Rovers parked up on a gravel driveway and a group of burly instructors, dressed head to toe in black like something out of *The Matrix*, climbed out and marched towards us. They were hardened, weathered men who were perfectly built for their surroundings. The blokes had no interest in exchanging pleasantries and immediately started barking orders at us. 'Drop your bags and get inside,' one of them shouted. 'Who do you think you're talking to?' I thought to myself. I was tired and irritable and my instinct was to react but I decided to keep quiet; I didn't fancy getting into a scuffle with any of them.

We all trudged inside a large dining hall for breakfast, with three long wooden tables for the players and staff. On the walls were stag busts from previous hunts on the estates. I wondered whether any of our heads would end up alongside them if we stepped out of line. Once we sat down, the day's schedule was explained to us. It quickly became apparent that they were going to try and break us. They didn't care about our ability with a football or what we'd done in our careers. In fact, some of them didn't even watch the game. Instead, the focus was on our personalities, mental strength and how we operated within a team. Were we selfish individuals or real team players? Our response to the challenges ahead would inform Keith who he could rely on in the winter months when the games were coming thick and fast or when we were going through a bad patch. I was determined to show him I could be counted on.

Our leader for the day was Phil Ercolano, a former football agent who had created the camp in the belief it would help to create successful players and people by testing their response to adversity in an alien environment. Along with his staff,

149

he'd devised ten outdoor challenges, which are available to clubs and individual players. Each one is built around 12 improvement pillars: mental strength, physical performance, team relationships, leadership, communication, self-belief, self-awareness, motivation, career-life balance, self-discipline, personal brand and values. Over breakfast, every player was asked to give themselves a score out of five for each pillar and would be required to do the same at the end of the camp. Some players tried to impress or maybe massage their own egos by giving themselves full marks in certain categories, while others marked themselves down, perhaps to reduce the level of expectancy on their shoulders. I was confident I would come through it, but I was interested to find out who my team-mates really were and how they'd react to what was to come. The day would tell me a lot about the dressing room I hoped to be a part of.

There was a light fog in the air and dew glistened on the lawns as we were given instructions about our first challenge, which involved a hill run from the camp to our first base. An instructor told each of us to set off at ten-second intervals and ordered us to chase the man in front. If we were all fit enough and worked hard enough, none of us should be caught. But to make things even harder, we also had to memorise the route and were warned that half a team of rugby players had spent several hours lost in the woods the previous summer after failing to listen properly. It was a run fuelled by fear. At regular intervals, I had a quick look over my shoulder to see if the guy behind me was making up ground. The terrain was gruelling. There were no purpose-built paths, just grass, country lanes and hills. It took about 15 minutes for me to reach the base, where I collapsed in a heap on the floor. The run was brutal and had left us all shell-shocked. A couple of hours ago we'd all been in bed, but now we were sweating profusely and fearing what was to come. It turned out the run was little more than a warm-up and there was no time to rest before the start of the next punishing stage.

In front of us was a seemingly impossible assault course of tyres, wooden logs, sandbags and barrels, like something you'd see on a world strongman competition on Channel Five, which we had to complete as fast as possible. There were three lanes, so each of us had to compete against two other team-mates before our individual times were recorded on a leaderboard. It was a test of strength and fitness, but also grit. I said to myself that I simply wouldn't give up. My mindset is that I'd rather injure myself and be forced to quit than to pull out because I'd given in. If my shoulder popped out and I had to stop then I could live with that, but if I gave up just because it was hard work then that would tell me I was mentally weak. The course became progressively more difficult and the harder it got, the more my muscles screamed at me to stop. After the pain I'd been through during chemotherapy, I just kept telling myself, 'it could be worse, Joe, it could be worse'. I also had the support of my team-mates cheering from the side and willing me on, which gave me more mental fuel. I posted a respectable time, which put me in the top five on the leaderboard, and I still felt I had plenty in the tank ahead of the afternoon challenges.

At lunch, I was wary of eating too much in case I was sick during the next set of tasks. I'd heard rumours about what we'd be doing and limited myself to a drink and a couple of bread rolls. I soon realised it was a wise move after we were led to the bottom of a large hill and told to carry a team-mate to the top, where the burly blokes were stood shouting and inwardly enjoying watching our struggle. I decided to pace myself like I used to in cross country and found a position nicely in the middle of the pack before picking people off one by one. Once I went past each one, I could see in their faces that they were gone.

In individual pursuits you have to run your own race and forget about what your competitors are doing. I used the same approach for the next challenge, which required us to run two miles up a peak while carrying a log above our heads. I was delighted to finish in third place, but Keith came up to me immediately afterwards and told me I'd slacked off. 'You could've won that, there was more in the tank.' He was probably right, and if I'd had another 500m to play with I would've fancied catching the two lads in front of me, but it was easy for him to say when he was stood at the finish line watching on!

I thought I'd done enough during the day to show my inner steel, but there was still one last stage for us to overcome and I was dreading it. Lake Windermere looked like an ocean as we stared out at the vast expanse of water in front of us. 'Is there anyone here who can't swim?' shouted one of the instructors. I put my hand up slowly in embarrassment, along with a couple of other lads. Swimming, in my opinion, is a skill a father teaches his child when they're growing up, but mine was never around and so I'd never learned. When I was at Rochdale, I had to use a float and kick my legs during a swimming session, much to the amusement of my team-mates.

Still, there was no chance of me being allowed to sit out the task. I was thrown a life jacket and told to swim out to a water buoy in the distance along with the rest of my team-mates. We then had to swim back to shore and run to the camp. At the start, I thrashed around in the water like a newborn duckling while everyone else started to disappear out of view. I knew how to keep myself afloat but moving forwards proved to be a bit trickier. Eventually I began to move, but it took me over 45 minutes to complete the task, long after the others had finished. The run was without question the hardest of my life. All my clothes were soaking wet and my arms and legs could barely co-ordinate. To make it even more difficult, an instructor was driving behind me in a Range Rover to make sure I kept a steady pace. I just focused on putting one foot in front of the other until I at last made it back.

The test was over, but Keith still wasn't happy. 'What would you do if your daughter was drowning at sea?' he asked me. I was about to reply but he interrupted. 'You need to learn how to swim, you need to be able to come to her rescue if she's in trouble.' He was right and so I promised him that I'd start taking swimming lessons on my days off. As the squad and coaching staff sat down for dinner, the purpose of the camp suddenly dawned on me. Nobody was scrolling through their smartphones or wearing headphones and listening to music. Instead, we were all talking and laughing about the day. We'd had an incredible shared experience, which had pulled us all together. We'd all leant on each other for moral support when we had to dig deep, which would serve us well in the season ahead. I already felt like I was part of the group and kept my fingers crossed that Keith had seen enough in me over the previous week to offer me a contract.

My experience at the camp made me realise more than ever that a player's brain dictates so much of his career, perhaps more so than the talent in his feet. The squad was made up of 20 or so lads who had all been the best players in their Sunday league and school teams but had at some point or another been blindsided by adversity. They could've given up and taken an easier path free of the potential pitfalls of elite sport, but they possessed the self-belief to continue and had made a career for themselves. I thought of some of the talented players I played with at United who had drifted out of the game, and now realised they just didn't have the mental mettle to make it. For some, being released would've dented their confidence beyond repair, while the pressure of going on trial to earn a contract would've proven too much for many others.

A few days after returning home to Rochdale, Keith called me with the news I'd been desperate to hear. He'd been impressed with my efforts the previous week and offered me a six-month contract on £600 a week. It still wasn't a lot, but the club also operated a sequence-based bonus scheme, which would top up my salary if we were successful. A three-game winning run would be worth £450, £150 per win, meaning I'd stand to make over £1,000 a week. I reported back to the boss, Chantelle, and she told me to go for it even though it meant I'd have to spend several days a week living in Carlisle, away from her and Lula. To save on the cost of renting a property, the club moved me into a house right next to their stadium with five other players; Michael Raynes, a French kid called Kevin Osei, Charlie Wyke, Jason Kennedy and Luke Joyce.

It was a great place to live. When I arrived with my suitcase, I felt like I was moving into student accommodation with a load of my mates. I had the top floor to myself and we all shared a kitchen and living area and decided we'd do a weekly shop like one big football family. Three of us had kids, so we were mature enough to respect our own individual routines and make it work. A few of us were also from the north-west, so we decided we'd take it in turns to drive back home on our days off and drop each other off on the way to save on petrol.

We were a mature bunch of lads who were keen to live disciplined lives and make a real go of the season ahead. But when you've got six blokes living under the same roof there are always going to be times when you act like big kids and there were certainly plenty of those, especially in the first few weeks. There were nerf gun fights and practical jokes aplenty, and I often felt like I had to sleep with one eye open in case someone had targeted me for revenge over a previous prank or just fancied a spontaneous joke at my expense. After an uncertain summer, I was ready to kick-start my career and prove I could still become the player I once promised to be.

Chapter 12
The tide

IT was like a scene from a horror film. A mass of water ripped through roads and fields like a tsunami, claiming everything in its path. A murky brown river carrying cars, freezers and memories swam through the city without remorse. Locals climbed in dinghies to escape, while others clung to their homes like lovers caught in a storm.

It was December 2015 and Storm Desmond had descended over Carlisle and deposited a month's worth of rainfall over the city in just 24 hours. The deluge had left Brunton Park, which is close to the Rivers Petteril, Eden and Caldew, drowning under eight feet of water. The crossbars at both ends of the pitch looked like they were fighting to stay afloat as the rain continued to fall. Thousands of people had been forced to evacuate their homes, while an even greater number were told they would be without power for days.

Spirits had been high on the team coach after a 5-0 victory over Welling United in the second round of the FA

Cup, where Charlie Wyke had bagged himself a hat-trick in a morale-boosting win. But on the journey home news filtered through of the devastation that awaited us upon our return to Carlisle. Incredibly, some of our supporters who had made the trip had done so despite knowing their homes would be partially underwater when they returned. This was far more important than 22 blokes kicking a ball around a pitch, and we decided there and then to help the local community by distributing food, water and blankets to those who had been worst affected.

The call to arms was led by our captain, Danny Grainger, who issued a rallying cry against Mother Nature as we watched the news on the coach televisions on the way home and sat open-mouthed as wave after wave of chaos rolled by. 'We need to help these people,' he said. 'I don't care how much or whatever it takes, but we have to help these people to get their bottom floors emptied. The people of this town have been there for us through our ups and downs and we must be there for them now.'

Danny was Mr Carlisle. He was a Cumbrian lad who was embedded in the local community and could feel the pain of the people more than others. He'd witnessed the impact of the floods when they'd hit the city in January 2005. Back then, two months of rainfall fell in one night, in what was described as a 'one in 200-year event' by experts. Flood defences were breached, leading to the deaths of three people and damage to 2,000 homes. The football club was devastated, but local residents had felt let down by the staff and players for failing to help with the clean-up job in the local area.

We couldn't let that happen again and decided we would get to work on Tuesday, to allow a couple of days for the water to subside and give the boys who lived in the area the chance to sort out their own homes. Our first-choice keeper, Mark Gillespie, hadn't travelled with us due to a virus and stayed behind to recover in one of the houses owned by the club. He was enjoying an afternoon nap but woke up to find water climbing up the stairs. He had to be rescued out of an upstairs window and rowed to safety. Our other keeper, Dan Hanford, had been due to move into a new house with his girlfriend, Suzi, but it was now underwater, while his white BMW was also wrecked. The back window had been smashed in and the force of Desmond had blown a green wheelie bin on top of his car. A suitcase full of his clothes had even been swept away by the current. Fortunately for me my wheels were on dry land back at our M6 pick-up point near Manchester, but our lads' pad hadn't escaped the damage and we were told we'd have to live in hotels for the foreseeable future, possibly until the end of the season. The possessions that were left at the house had been destroyed.

The club identified four homes that looked to have been worst hit by the weather. Led by Danny and Keith, 15 of us split into groups, so we pulled on wellies, rubber gloves and industrial cleaning masks and got to work. Me, Charlie, Luke Joyce, Raynesy and Jason Kennedy helped to salvage possessions from the property of 73-year-old Bill Douthwaite, a lifelong Carlisle fan who told us he'd been rescued from his home in a floating fridge freezer a few days earlier. We also visited his neighbour, Angela Watson, who hilariously told us she'd saved her season ticket from the rising water but realised later on she'd forgotten to pick up her husband's wallet and medication.

I couldn't believe how positive the local people were given what had just happened. I remember being stood in the kitchen of another home, with water up to my knees. I could see pictures from family photo albums floating from room to room. I tried to salvage a few but they were soaked beyond repair. You can replace household items but photographs carry sentimental value. Memories had literally been washed away. It was heartbreaking and I couldn't help but feel sorry for everyone that had been affected. One woman who lived there had been through the same process ten years earlier and it had changed her outlook on life. 'We've come through it once and we'll come through it again,' she said with a shrug of her shoulders. I admired her resilience and wondered if I could've been quite so philosophical if my home had been flooded twice in a decade.

In the end, we realised there were more people that desperately needed our help. That day, we managed to empty 15 properties. It was an awful experience but a valuable one as well. I'll always find money for nice clothes and justify purchasing the latest trainers, but I've never been materialistic and it hammered home to me how disposable your possessions really are. In the end, it's only the people you're close to that really matter. Some of the locals had lost thousands of pounds worth of valuables, sofas, TVs, microwaves and various other goods, but they hadn't lost their loved ones and for that they were thankful.

The following day something remarkable happened as the water subsided and the sun emerged from behind the clouds. The residents we'd helped, plus many more supporters, queued up outside Brunton Park eager to help with the clear-up operation at the stadium. Some of them had no insurance and had literally lost everything, but to them the club was a symbol of the local community and they wouldn't allow it to rot. They tried to minimise the damage by rooting through the offices and dressing rooms, but there was nothing they could do about the pitch, though two goldfish were apparently rescued and reunited with their owners. The surface had always been a carpet and a dream to play on, but now it was in a state of disrepair and it looked like it would be months before we'd set foot on it again.

However, the city was alive with community spirit and a few hours later 22 wagons, emblazoned with the name of the local haulier, Eddie Stobart, on the side, pulled up outside the stadium with a special delivery. Each wagon was packed with rolls of new turf. Carlisle's head groundsman at the time, Dave Mitchell, is known as one of the best in the business and he immediately started digging up the sodden turf and rolling and kneading out the new stuff like a master baker working with fresh warm dough. It was a moving day that warmed my heart. A city had come together as one to help each other in their hour of need.

On 23 January, nearly two months after Desmond had devastated Carlisle, we made an emotional return to Brunton Park to face York City. During that period we'd played our home games 90 miles away on borrowed pitches at Preston,

Blackpool and Blackburn, and our fans had followed us in vast numbers. It was good to be home at last and give them something in return for their commitment to the cause. Ironically, the visitors had also been hit hard by storm damage and so local journalists decided to christen the game 'The Flood Derby'. The stadium was packed as fans came in their hordes to say thank you to the club for their help before Christmas. In the modern game, so many clubs are disconnected from their fanbase, because they treat them like nothing more than customers, so it was incredible to see the special bond that had formed between supporters and the team. They sang their hearts out that day, and even though we were held to a 1-1 draw, the afternoon was a victory for everyone involved. It was humbling to be part of it.

The tide had turned and not just for Carlisle. After my experiences at Cassius Camps, I'd taken Keith's advice on board and used my spare time during the week wisely by spending several afternoons a week learning how to swim at a nearby leisure centre. I didn't hire an instructor; instead, I started by learning basic strokes with a float and then once I had enough confidence, began swimming lengths of the pool. Granted, I'd learned about 20 years later than I should have done, but I was happy to have done so at last and felt confident I could now look after Lula if, as Keith pointed out, she was to ever find herself in any sort of danger in the water.

Still, I was far more comfortable on grass. I made my debut in a 4-4 draw against Cambridge United in our second league game of the season. It was one of the most emotionally draining games I've ever experienced, as momentum swung back and forth like a pendulum. The following week I scored my first goal since returning from cancer on a Tuesday night trip to Plymouth. We lost 4-1, and it was a terrible team performance, but I felt like a weight had been lifted off my shoulders. It had been over 12 months since I'd last hit the back of the net and until that moment I didn't truly feel like I was back. I didn't start every week, but I featured regularly up until Christmas when my six-month deal was due to expire. I felt I'd won Keith's trust and was confident I'd be offered another contract until the end of the season, but I very nearly undid all my good work shortly before the floods hit in December.

It was a Friday afternoon and me and the rest of the boys in the house were relaxing after training, ahead of our game the following day. But we also had another important event in the football calendar to prepare for, the annual Christmas party. The squad had decided to go to Edinburgh for a good knees-up after the Crawley game to celebrate a positive first half of the season, which had left us well placed to mount a push for the play-offs. We stopped off at the shops after training to buy a few beers and put them in the fridge to chill. All of our going out gear was ironed and hung up on a big rail ready in the back room so we could put it in our suitcases and have a couple of beers on the train up to Edinburgh.

Suddenly the front door swung open. 'Afternoon gentlemen, how are we doing?' asked a familiar voice. Shit. It was Keith Curle. He'd walked in without knocking and was heading for the living room. I picked up the rail with our clothes on and chucked it over the other side of the sofa. There was a dart board near the table, so two of us pretended we were playing a game of arrows to guard our stash of ale. 'So, this is how you spend your afternoons, is it?' he laughed, as he saw us throwing darts into the board. 'Yeah, yeah, gaffer,' I replied, trying to disguise my fear. 'I thought I'd come and check that you're looking after this place,' he said. 'The cleaner says she doesn't have much to do, you keep it pretty clean and tidy.' We all agreed with him and carried on playing, while inwardly praying he didn't ask to see the inside of the fridge, where our crate was chilling.

He made a bit more small talk and then went upstairs to have a look around the bedrooms before deciding he was satisfied with his inspection. He told us to get an early night ahead of the game and then left. As soon as the door shut we all collapsed on the floor laughing. We were so relieved we'd got away with it, having been metres away from being rumbled. If he'd found the beers I'm certain he would've gone mental and accused us of not focusing on the game. Who knows, he might've even separated us like naughty schoolboys at the back of the class. It was one of many funny memories I've got of living in that house. Pranks happened on a daily basis. On one occasion, Charlie thought it'd be hilarious to tip my bed up with me still in it, just after I'd turned the light off and gone to bed. I threatened him with revenge but he didn't listen, none of them did, nobody was ever safe. All the lads were professional when it came down to football, but I felt like I was sampling university life without the midweek booze-ups. Sadly, the floods meant we had to move from hotel to hotel until the final weeks of the season, which meant our little family unit was broken up, but we at least had the memories.

I'd done everything that had been asked of me and Keith rewarded me with another six-month contract in January, which took me up until the end of the season. My relationship with him was the best I'd had with a manager since my days working under Keith Hill. I knew we'd get on from the moment I first met him when I arrived at the training ground. I remember watching him as a player and he was a fierce competitor but as a manager he'd often bottle up his rage. If you continuously bollock players the impact wears off and I think he was aware of that. I'd sensed that we'd been close to seeing his angry side come out on a couple of occasions after poor performances and got the feeling he wouldn't be able to contain it forever. It turned out I was right.

Players and managers all have their own peculiar habits and Keith was no different. Before every game he liked his dressing room to be organised in a very specific fashion. His habits were bordering on OCD. In his head, a clear dressing room meant a clear mind. After a dismal 1-0 defeat away to Newport, on a freezing February afternoon on a terrible pitch, he noticed that something was out of place. The kitman and Lee Fearn, our physical conditioning coach, had made the mistake of having a tidy up and had moved things from their normal stations. It tipped him over the edge. 'Why are all those protein shakes in the middle?!' he shouted, pointing at the plastic shakers sat on the table. Nobody dared to say a word. I knew that any moment they were about to go everywhere. Seconds later he erupted and started throwing shakes all over the dressing room. Nobody escaped. There was pink liquid splattered over everyone. He wasn't done there. He grabbed a basket full of GPS monitors and began launching them at everyone, bouncing them off the floor and walls. Everyone was ducking and diving in the corner like a boxer trying to slip punches.

There was a stunned silence, before he began his verbal attack. 'None of you have got the bollocks to get up and say anything because you know I'll bite your fucking face off,' he screamed. 'I'm fucking right and you know it, you tossed it off, not one of you fancied it today!' He used to play for Wimbledon during the Crazy Gang era and now I could see why he fitted right in. Sometimes you feel hard done to when a manager has a go at you, particularly if you've just been beaten by a better team, but on this occasion our performance had been dreadful and he was right to be livid. The coach journey home felt like a funeral procession. Keith had the respect of everyone, but he definitely had more power after that dressing down because his reaction had come as such a shock. I secretly loved it. Nobody wanted to risk another bollocking and it was no surprise that we went on a good run in the aftermath of that game.

Unfortunately I found myself on the bench as the season drew to a close, though I was happy with my performance on the final day, as we thumped Notts County 5-0. Keith had been sacked by the club a couple of years earlier and I could tell that result meant a lot to him. He'd stuck two fingers up to them and showed them what he was capable of. As a squad, it was a display that highlighted how much we were behind him. There was no chance of us switching off and coasting through the final 90 minutes, we wanted to get that win for him and made sure it was emphatic. The result also gave us momentum heading into the next season.

We finished in tenth place in League Two, which was a successful season given the club had narrowly avoided relegation the previous year, as well as the impact of the floods. At our end-of-season awards night, everyone came together to celebrate the campaign, which had seen both the club and local community come through great adversity. After the prizes had been handed out, Keith came over to have a word. 'So, what are you thinking then?' he asked me. I told him I was going to enjoy the night, because it was potentially my last with the group, but we agreed to meet the following day. My contract was about to expire and I needed to make a decision about my future. A day later he laid his cards out on the table. 'I could offer you another 12-month contract, but I can't guarantee that you'd be in my starting 11 and I think you want more now you've found your feet,' he said. He told me he saw me as a striker in a 4-4-2 or a 3-5-2, but Jabo Ibehre and Charlie Wyke would be his first-choice partnership and I'd be the first substitute off the bench.

I was grateful for his honesty and happy that we were on the same wavelength. I'd spent the last two years rebuilding my mind and body and had been in and out of two different teams. I was ready to play football every week and it was time for me to go somewhere where I could do that. He understood and told me how amazing it had been to see the impact I'd made on the dressing room and the respect I had from all the players and staff. I thanked him for taking a chance on me and more importantly giving me my confidence back. We shook hands and left on good terms. It was probably the best one-on-one chat I've ever had with a manager and showed just how good he was at dealing with players individually; he'd made me feel valued even when delivering bad news.

Towards the end of the season me and the boys had moved back into our house but now I had to pack my bags again and leave for good. We'd spent so much time together in the house and in the car driving up and down the motorway, and had become really close. This was the end of the road for our little football family and we all started to well up as we put our suitcases in the boot and started the drive back to Manchester.

For the first time since I'd been at Rochdale, I'd felt like I was a key part of a dressing room and had forged genuine friendships with several of the lads. I'd only been there for a year, but we'd been through so much together. The camp in the Lake District had pushed us to our limits and then everyone had pulled together during the floods. The club and local community had become one and I felt privileged to have been part of that story. The storm had passed and it was time to chase the sun.

Chapter 13

Chasing the sun

THE start of my stag do was like a scene from *The Hangover*, as me and nine of my closest friends met at Manchester Airport at the crack of dawn and steeled ourselves for five days of mayhem. At least there ought to have been nine, but we were already one man down. My mate Matt missed his taxi, meaning he faced a race against time to make the flight. There was also another problem; Lloydy had forgotten to fill in his ESTA form and wouldn't be allowed to fly without it.

He called his personal assistant, Joanne, who had sorted out all his travel bookings in the past. He asked her why she hadn't done the form, but she wasn't taking any of his rubbish and told him it was his responsibility, having already sorted his flights and accommodation. Reuben started filling in his details on his mobile phone in the hope we could complete it in time before we jetted off. He was under pressure, but he works as an accountant and handles big-money deals on a daily basis, so he was the perfect person to have on hand as we waited at the check-in desk.

It was a revealing few minutes. For years, Lloydy had insisted he was 39, but we had a suspicion he was hiding the truth. 'Fine, I'm 46, but I'm 39 to you,' he said. We all started laughing. I'd seen him tell so many people over the years that he was 39 with a big beaming smile made brighter by an expensive set of veneers. Now we knew his true identity at last, we faced a nerve-wracking wait to see if he'd be let on the plane. As he placed his passport on the scanner, we all held our breath and watched the dial on the screen go round and round like a roulette wheel.

My proposal to Chantelle in Dubai 12 months earlier had been equally nerve-wracking. The day before I got down on one knee, I visited a nearby restaurant to plan the big moment with the staff and my close friend Yas. I'm not normally one for romance, but the plan was for a crystal ball to be brought out with dessert in a plume of smoke. Hidden inside would be the box containing the engagement ring. I had to leave the ring with the staff overnight, but the fear of them losing it or my cunning plan not coming off meant I didn't sleep a wink. Chantelle slept soundly, blissfully unaware of what was about to happen.

Twenty-four hours later, my worst nightmare nearly materialised. She looked a million dollars and we both had a brilliant meal, but she was adamant she didn't want a dessert. Our waitress intervened. 'The chef insists you try something, we'll bring it out,' she said. I was a nervous wreck trying to hold it together. She returned a few minutes later and placed the crystal ball on the table. Through the smoke I could see her smiling and before I had a chance to go down on one knee, she dived into the box. 'Yes, yes, yes!' she said. 'I take it you want to be my wife?' I laughed. We were both ecstatic and I rang her parents a short while later to tell them the news. I deliberately proposed on Father's Day as a gift to her dad, but also because it was an occasion that I could only celebrate as a result of her bringing Lula into this world safe and sound.

Our plan had been to get married two years later, but we brought the wedding forward 12 months after Chantelle's dad fell seriously ill. When I first met Paul, he was a real man's man, strong and full of life, but fibrosis of the lungs had left him weak and reliant on oxygen cylinders just to be able to breathe normally. He was a proud Yorkshireman, but he moved to Manchester from Hull to be closer to his family. When she went on her hen do, I moved in with him and saw the full extent of his suffering.

I spent a week in the life of Chantelle's mum, Anita. She's an angel and never complained once about the burden of caring for him, even though it must've been physically and mentally draining. He was out of breath all the time and didn't even have the energy to cook for himself. It was horrible to see. I could tell that he felt embarrassed at having to ask me to pass him the remote or get something from the fridge. Lula was only three, but she could sense he was ill and sat on his lap and watched TV with him. She didn't misbehave once and it was incredible to see how in tune she was with his situation.

As much as I hated seeing him in pain, I'm so happy that we spent that quality time together, and I think he appreciated having another man around the house, having been surrounded by women for so much of his life. We had some deep chats about life and he told me he'd have passed away a long time ago had it not been for Lula. He looked forward to her coming to visit him every weekend and felt energised by her playfulness. His only regret was that the weekend always seemed to pass by so quickly. In his eyes, she could do no wrong. She was his angel. If anyone told her off he'd tell them to leave her alone and stop being nasty. Lula would take full advantage and immediately back him up: 'Yeah Gangan, tell them!'

I read an article recently about a new initiative at old people's homes in America. Once or twice a week they take young kids to visit and engage the residents' brains. It reminded me of the impact Lula had on Paul. My grandma, who has been ravaged by dementia for a couple of years now, also seems to have benefited from her presence. She's forgotten my name and pretty much everyone else's in the family, but she still remembers Lula's. Although I was at a different stage of my life, she had been my motivation during my battle with cancer. When I was at my lowest ebb, throwing up repeatedly, I was driven on by the thought of making more memories with her. There's something infectious about youthful promise that breathes new life into your world.

Three years had passed since I'd been given the all-clear, but cancer still hovered over our family like a cloud. A few months earlier, my uncle Terry had passed away following a long battle with bowel cancer. I went to see him at a hospice in Bath, where patients who have failed to respond to treatment effectively go to die. He was sat in a wheelchair and was almost unrecognisable. His legs were full of fluid because his body was shutting down and the rest of his body resembled a skeleton. Chantelle burst out crying when she saw him.

I wheeled him outside to a bench so we could have a talk in private. 'Do you fancy pushing me all the way down the hill?' he joked. Despite how sick he was, he retained his sense of humour. He loved football and was proud of what I'd achieved, having followed my career from the very beginning. One of my earliest memories is playing football with him and some friends at a park in Bath. I nutmegged him and ran through on goal, but out of nowhere he swiped my legs from underneath me, leaving me in tears. His competitive streak went too far that day, but I laugh about it now and his desire to win was infectious.

At his funeral I was overcome with a sense of guilt. We both had cancer at similar times but he'd gone in one direction and I'd gone in another. As I carried his coffin into church with Reuben, I glanced at family and friends and felt like I was witnessing what could've happened to me. I pulled myself together and managed to do a small reading during the service. His passing broke my mum and Nicey's heart. They'd all been close and their lives would never be the same again. But despite everything, there was still so much to celebrate. Me and Chantelle were going to get married but first we had to get through airport security and survive the bright lights of Vegas.

I could almost see the sweat on Lloydy's brow as he looked at the scanner and waited to find out if he'd be let through. After what seemed like an age, the gates opened and he walked through a free man. His details had been processed just in the nick of time. A short while later, Matt came sprinting through and joined the group. We were only a couple of hours into the stag do but it was already carnage. We all headed to a lounge, where we had a drink and a bit of breakfast and the boys got to know each other. I knew them all individually; they were a combination of ex-team-mates, schoolmates and family friends, but they hadn't mixed as a group before. Lloydy's revelation about his true age was a nice shared experience to get everyone going and he continued to justify his big lie. 'I struggled to accept it when I turned 45, but I reckon I'll be fine when I get to 49.'

I'd told the boys to bring £2,000 each, but after my first trip to Vegas I knew that figure could easily double. We were staying at the Cosmopolitan Hotel, which was slap bang in the centre of Vegas. I calculated that we'd need £400 to £500 a day for a pool party in the day and then a nightclub. We ended up doing a fair bit more than that. Paul McGovern was the first casualty of the trip and pulled out of the opening night out after complaining of an upset stomach. He was the butt of the jokes for the rest of the trip. On the Saturday we went to a pool party at Wet Republic to watch Calvin Harris, but I could tell the pace was already catching up with Lloydy. It was a baking hot day and the set was due to start at 3pm but the crowd were told he was running late. 'Nobody makes Gary G wait 15 minutes. It's baking hot, I've drank far too much, I'm going.' For some reason, he'd decided to change his name from Gary Lloyd to Gary G, his Vegas alter ego. It was bizarre, but that was him.

He stormed off and disappeared through the crowds, but 45 minutes later he called me to say he couldn't find the exit of the MGM Grand. 'How the fuck do I get out of here?' He said. 'I've been going round and round in circles.' I could hear an American accent giving him directions on the other end of the phone and a few seconds later he put the phone down. We saw him when we got back to our hotel later that afternoon and let him know that he'd missed an amazing day. It's funny seeing how people react to the relentless pace of a stag do, and I could tell he was on his last legs. 'Tomorrow night is going to be my last night mate,' he told me. 'Don't tell the other lads, I'm just going to get off. But I'll see you when you get to Ibiza.'

We planned to hit Saturday night hard and Lloydy was on a mission to go out in style. We went to a club called Jewel to watch the rapper Swizz Beatz. We'd all clubbed together and paid for a table, but Lloydy still wasn't happy with where we were sat, because he couldn't see the stage. He called one of the promoters over and demanded that we were moved to a better table. 'I'm sorry, sir, the tables over there cost $10,000 more than this table,' said a guy in a suit. 'Fine, I'll pay it,' he replied. I was stunned. 'Lloydy, are you sure mate?' I said. He was insistent. 'I'm probably never going to come back here, so I'm going to do it my way,' he said. I couldn't believe he'd just forked out for it like he was ordering a bottle of beer at the bar. That table must have taken his total spending on the trip to £20,000. About half an hour later, the table service arrived, with sparklers coming out of the drinks and a big banner with the name 'Gary G' plastered across it.

It was one of the best nights of my life. I looked around at my boys all having an amazing time and felt proud that they'd made such a huge effort to come to Vegas and celebrate. Lloydy was in his element; the sparklers and banner weren't really my thing but I was happy he was having a good time. He'd been like a dad to me since we'd first met when I was 18 and he was still by my side, ready to watch me start a new chapter in my life. Before the night was over, a few of us went to the toilet for a pit stop. Out of nowhere, Neymar walked past and headed inside one of the cubicles. 'Boys, we do not let him out of here without getting a picture,' I said. 'I want a deep block, men behind the ball, he isn't getting past us.' When he came out he stopped for a picture and then dropped his shoulder like he'd done past countless defenders on the pitch and disappeared into the darkness of the club.

It was the perfect way to end the trip. We'd managed to man-mark Neymar in a nightclub toilet but getting everyone on the plane back proved more difficult. We had to fly from Vegas to Chicago before flying back to Manchester. If we didn't make the flight we'd face a race to get to Ibiza in time for my wedding, which was only a few days away. When we arrived at Chicago airport, a voice over the tannoy sent us into a panic. 'Please would Mr Thompson and his party go to Gate B59, this is your final boarding call.' We were all drained and hungover but we mustered the energy to sprint through the airport. However, Nicky Blackman, who had been nursing a knee injury all year, refused to run. Knowing Nicky, I reckon he was secretly hoping he'd miss the flight so he could stay behind and see what Chicago had to offer for 24 hours. Luckily, we managed to have a word with the plane crew, who waited a few minutes longer for him to board. Within minutes of finding our seats, we were all fast asleep as we tried to recover from a brutal few days.

A few days later, the big day arrived. I'd always wanted to get married abroad. Part of me wanted to see who would go the extra mile and fly out to watch us tie the knot. We were joined by 65 guests in San Miguel, which is in the north of Ibiza island, away from all the clubs and bars. Getting Paul on the plane was like a military operation. His cylinders had to have the right amount of oxygen in them and we were concerned that they might be affected by the change of air pressure in the cabin during the flight. Fortunately, he was fine and he felt a lot better in the warmth of Spain. We'd flown out a few times during the season to make sure everything was in place and now all I needed was for Chantelle to turn up and say 'I do'.

The ceremony was due to start at 1pm, but in typical Chantelle fashion, she was 20 minutes late getting to the church. I wasn't worried she wouldn't show up, that's the way she's always been. If we go to a restaurant I'll book it for 8:30pm and tell her we need to be there for 8pm because I know she's always on the last minute. Eventually, she came walking down the aisle with Paul and Lula on either side. She looked absolutely stunning. I was so happy we'd brought the wedding forward so that Paul could be there to see Chantelle get married. 'It's over to you now, look after her,' he said to me at the altar. I knew he'd used every last ounce of his energy just to walk her down the aisle and was literally handing her over to me to look after her.

I was still hoarse after five days of partying in Vegas, but thankfully held out long enough for me to say my vows. Afterwards we all headed back to the villa for the speeches, before dancing the night away. During my speech I did my best to frighten the lads who had been on my stag do by telling them all to stand up like a police identity parade. They were petrified and exchanged nervous glances while their girlfriends and wives looked on waiting to see what stories I had to tell. 'Don't worry lads,' I said. 'I just want to thank you for making my time in Vegas perfect, I couldn't have asked for more.' I could tell they were all relieved when they sat down with their pride and relationships still intact.

I mentioned my dad briefly, who had just been released on tag for assault and battery, and explained that he was unable to attend due to his 7pm curfew and a court order banning him from leaving the country. It was dark humour, but everyone was howling with laughter. In my haste I forgot to read out my passage thanking Nicey for everything she'd done for me over the years. Midway through the night my cousins mentioned that I hadn't really mentioned Nicey and it was only then that I realised my mistake. I was horrified and asked the DJ to stop the music. For the first time during the whole wedding I burst out crying as I told everyone what a rock she'd been for me and the rest of the family over the years. I know she hates attention but I couldn't let that moment pass without acknowledging her role in my life.

The rest of the night was like a dream. Everyone danced the night away and loads of us ended up jumping in the villa pool, including Chantelle in her wedding dress. I dread to think how many pounds worth of material was soaking in the water, and I've never asked her since. I made sure I enjoyed the moment and smiled as I looked around at everyone having a great time. My mum must have been so proud that day given the daily battles she faced just to make ends meet when we were kids, on top of her own struggles with mental illness. She did an amazing job bringing us up, and in the end her two sons had turned out ok.

I often watch our wedding video to remind myself how amazing our special day was. We only decided to get it filmed about a week before the wedding and it was one of the best decisions we've made. We hired a young lad called Cameron and he did such a good job; he's since worked on weddings for loads of other footballers, including Manchester United defender Chris Smalling and Sheffield Wednesday's Liam Palmer. Over 100,000 people have now watched our video on Facebook and we occasionally get strangers coming up to us in random places asking us if we're the couple from the Facebook wedding video. I can confirm that we are.

We spent a week in Ibiza, squeezing every last ounce of happiness out of our wedding. I'd never felt as content with life as I did during those seven days. It had been a dark few years for the whole family but we were stronger for it, and at last I felt we'd come out of the other side. Ibiza was the light at the end of the tunnel.

Chapter 14
Christmas is cancelled

I FELT like I was waking up from a dream as the plane touched down on the runway at Manchester Airport and shuddered to a halt. I rubbed the sleep from my eyes and realised I was an unemployed footballer again, but I wasn't worried like I had been in previous years. I'd been in this position before and felt I'd done enough to show I could still cut it in the Football League. But finding a new employer proved to be more difficult than I thought.

A few weeks after returning to normality, the only concrete interest had come from non-league side Barrow. It was better than nothing, I thought, so I spent a week training with them to get a feel for the club and work on my fitness. They trained in Manchester, which was convenient, but it was a huge drop in professionalism compared to what I'd been used to, and I was convinced I still had plenty to offer at a higher level. I pestered Lloydy for news but the clubs who had been in touch were up in Scotland, and I didn't want to uproot my family, particularly after the stress of the last few years. Lloydy was honest with me about the situation and told me to speak to other agents to see if they could help, even though it meant he wouldn't get a fee.

The way in which players find new clubs and win contracts has changed a lot since I started out. I know several lads who have been signed after putting together highlights packages and posting them on social media or even LinkedIn. You have to be active now and put yourself in the shop window. If a coach needs to get a player in quickly and you've got a well-edited video of yourself in action then it gives him an immediate idea of what you can offer. It also saves him the hassle of being misled by agents claiming to have a client who is the next big thing, only to find out that he's anything but. It isn't something I've had to do yet myself, but social media has become a great platform to showcase your talents and advertise your availability.

One afternoon I was at a play centre with Lula when Chantelle and my mum ordered me to ring Keith Hill. I was reluctant to go cap in hand to my former manager. I know a few players who have had great spells at clubs but then things have turned sour on their return. They expected to go back and everything to fall into place like it used to be, but then couldn't adapt to a new manager and team-mates. I'd made some amazing memories at Rochdale and didn't want to ruin them or taint my reputation in the eyes of the fans if my second spell wasn't as successful as my first. I was also wary of the stick I might get if things weren't going well when I lived close to the club. People love to rub it in and I was fearful of things not going to plan.

I explained my concerns to Chantelle, but she was persistent, and so was my mum, so I picked up the phone and gave him a call. 'What are you doing with yourself? You do know pre-season has already started?' he said to me in typical Keith fashion. I told him I was basically a househusband. 'You don't want to be doing that, Joe, it'll mess with your masculinity,' he joked. He said I could join his squad for pre-season training but added firmly that there was no guarantee I'd be offered a contract. I've never been given anything that I haven't worked for and didn't expect any favours from him. I was on trial again, just as I'd been after leaving Manchester United all those years ago.

I'd forgotten how hard training was under Keith, and it was a shock to the system after Vegas and Ibiza. I trained for three weeks without playing a pre-season game, but he could see that my fitness was good and I was ready to compete. We sat down in his office and he offered me a six-month contract on £500 a week. The wage was a pittance for a League One player. 'I want to see how hungry you are,' he said. 'Ohh I'll be hungry, I'll be eating baked beans on toast at this rate,' I replied. I had nothing else on the table, but I thought I'd try and make him sweat. 'I'll think about it,' I said.

I'd been driving for about five minutes when Lloydy called me. 'Where are you? Tell me you're still at the ground,' he said with urgency. I explained that I'd had a chat with the gaffer and was going home to think about the offer in the hope I could squeeze another couple of hundred quid a month out of him. 'I've spoken to Keith, if you don't sign it in a couple of days he'll withdraw the offer,' he said. 'He's calling your bluff, mate,' I replied. 'I can tell by his tone of voice that he isn't, turn around and sign the contract,' he ordered. I sighed and did as I was told. 'I'll show Keith how hungry I am,' I thought to myself. Ten minutes later I was a Rochdale player again. As always, Keith had won the battle of wills.

I wasn't happy with my salary, but on the pitch everything was rosy. We made a flying start to the season and I played a lot of football. The only thing missing from my game was goals, and I scored my first since my return in a 3-2 win over Scunthorpe, who were flying in the league. I was named man of the match, and the win saw us move into fourth place in League One. It was December, which meant it was Christmas party time again, and after the game we all headed to Newcastle to let our hair down. I had even more reason to celebrate. Keith had handed me an 18-month deal a few days earlier as a reward for my efforts. I was relieved to have some financial security at last, which meant I could now just focus on my football.

It was a two-day trip, but I had to return to Manchester a day earlier than the rest of the boys to make sure I was in a fit state for a check-up scan at Christie Hospital on the Monday morning. It was nothing to be worried about, it was a routine procedure. Normally cancer survivors undergo these scans every six months in the first two years after their treatment, but after my first diagnosis I'd undergone a trial to help with research, which meant I had to have one final scan three years after my initial diagnosis. I felt fitter and healthier than I'd ever been but ten days after they'd taken one last look at me, the hospital called and asked me to go back for a PET scan, which gives doctors a more detailed view of your insides. It unnerved me, but I had no reason to fear there was a problem because I had no symptoms and quickly buried the concerns in my head.

The nurses injected me with a red dye, which is made out of a radioactive glucose. If you have cancerous cells in your body, the dye makes them light up like a Christmas tree when you're inside the MRI scanner. I drifted in and out of sleep as I lay inside the scanner for nearly an hour, but my mind was racing. I kept thinking of the worst-case scenario, but I reminded myself that the odds were stacked in my favour. If you get past the two-year mark after remission, which I had done, then there is little chance of your cancer returning. I was also a healthy athlete, so what did I have to worry about? I was told that I would need to go back to the hospital a week later, on Christmas Eve of all days, to get my results.

I reassured everyone at the club that I was fine and returned to Christie Hospital for my appointment fully expecting to have a brief 15-minute chat, leave with a clean bill of health and head to training straight after. Chantelle drove me there and we took a seat in Dr Gibbs's office, who had been part of the team of experts who had overseen my first battle with cancer. I could tell by the look on his face that something was wrong. 'I'm really sorry to have to tell you this Joe, but we've found a cancerous tumour on your chest and it's showing signs of growth,' he said. 'I'm so, so sorry.'

I burst into tears. They were angry tears. I wanted to smash the room up. 'What do you mean, one fucking tumour, you've got to be kidding me?' I said. 'You didn't get rid of it the first time, did you?' He explained that my original treatment had been a success but I'd suffered a relapse. The tumour was a centimetre and a half in size but it was spreading towards my lymph nodes again. He told me there was cause for optimism because I had the same type of cancer as before and it hadn't attacked a major organ. I didn't care. I'd been told there was less than a 5 per cent chance of it coming back and didn't want to hear about statistics and platitudes. 'Don't try and tell me there's good news, because there's no fucking good news,' I wailed at him.

I could tell that he was finding the situation incredibly difficult having seen me go through my treatment the first time around. He explained that it was likely I'd have to wait several months before the treatment would start. 'I'm not sitting around waiting again,' I said. 'Calm down,' he replied. 'It's easy for you to say calm down,' I said. This time around I would need a more potent form of chemotherapy to try and eradicate the cancer for good, which would involve 24-hour cycles for six days, every other week, until they were confident it was gone. It was that powerful I would also require a stem cell transplant, to replenish my body with red and white blood cells, which would be killed by the dosage, and rebuild my immune system.

I felt like I'd buried an enemy, but they had climbed out of the ground and clawed me back. I didn't know how I was going to explain to Lula what was happening. Last time, she had only been a baby, but now she was old enough to ask questions. I knew that this time I would lose all of my hair and probably a substantial amount of weight. I wouldn't look like the dad she knew. I was worried what impact that would have on her psychologically. There was no way I could hide it from her. No child should have to see their mum or dad suffer with a serious illness, not at her age, but I knew I couldn't hide the truth from her. I'd have to be honest and find a way to break the news without frightening her.

I also had to tell Rochdale, who had just given me a new contract, that I might never play football again. We got in the car and I started punching the dashboard in anger. I was meant to be training on Christmas Day ahead of a game on Boxing Day, but after Chantelle had managed to calm me down I called Keith to tell him the news. I could barely string a sentence together and started crying over the phone. He told me to come to the training ground that afternoon so we could talk. It's only a short drive from Christie Hospital, so me and Chantelle headed for a coffee before we went to see him.

When I arrived, I bumped into Jimmy McNulty in the car park as he was leaving. It was déjà vu. He was the first person I saw the first time around when I went into Tranmere to tell the lads. I just started crying and he gave me a massive hug. The rest of the boys were finishing off a gym session inside. 'It's back boys, I've got cancer again,' I said. I felt terrible putting them in that position. What do you say to somebody who has just told you that? They told me they knew something had happened because Keith had been behaving like a man possessed, screaming and shouting at any little mistake. They did their best to make me feel better but we all knew I was in the shit.

Keith was waiting for me in his office along with a few of the other coaching staff. I did my best to relay to them what the doctor had said and told them I didn't want to play on Boxing Day, but they already had a plan to raise my spirits. 'Don't just stop now,' said Keith. 'You've got time before you start treatment; if you do nothing you'll just overthink everything. Let's get you fitter and stronger and better prepared for it.' It was a good way of thinking about it. I still felt completely normal and didn't have any symptoms. If I spent weeks sat on the sofa feeling sorry for myself and worrying, then mentally I would already have let cancer win the first round of our fight. We agreed that I'd train and play as normal until I felt I was no longer able to or my doctor intervened.

Incredibly, I continued to play for another three months, but still I kept the news a secret. Nobody outside of Rochdale or my closest family and friends knew I was running around with something growing and eating away at my insides, trying to kill me. I treated every training session, gym workout and game as a battle between me and cancer. Each one that I came through was another point in the bank and another wall of strength that the disease would have to try and topple. The competitive beast inside me had kicked in again and I wasn't going down without a fight. It's a character trait that can be draining at times, when you have this constant need to be number one. But at that moment I was thankful I had that spirit coursing through my veins because it was the perfect mental remedy against cancer.

Less than two weeks after my diagnosis, I scored in a league game away at Walsall. It wasn't the best goal of my career but at that point it was the most important. As the ball hit the back of the net I felt a rush of ecstasy and relief that is difficult to describe. 'You can still fucking do this,' I said to myself. It gave me a huge mental boost and for a brief while I felt strangely invincible. I was playing League One football and scoring goals while my body was battling cancer. If I could do that, I could do anything. Defenders would try to wind me up and get under my skin with a late tackle or a bit of off-the-ball chat but they were wasting their time. They couldn't dish out anything more harmful than what I was already fighting.

Keith continued to keep tabs on me like an over-protective parent looking after a sickly child. Every day he asked me if I still felt ok and was capable of playing another game. He was brilliant with me but after a while I began to lose patience with his constant questioning. 'I'm fine, let me crack on,' I snapped. I didn't mean to lose my cool, but football bravado had kicked in again. I knew that he had my best interests at heart, but I didn't want to be seen as a weak link and lose the trust of my team-mates. The game was keeping my mind and body healthy and if I gave him any reason to leave me out I feared it would kill my momentum.

March came and I was amazed that I still hadn't experienced any symptoms. There were no night sweats or feverish fluctuations in my temperature. But out of nowhere everything came crashing to a halt. I was named on the bench to face MK Dons, but after 25 minutes I replaced Steven Davies, who had limped off with a calf injury. As soon as I started running I felt horrendous. Just like last time, everyone else around me seemed to be moving at 100mph while I was moving in slow motion. I remember receiving a perfect drilled pass to my feet on the right wing, but for some reason I couldn't pick up the flight of the ball. It was like I had blurred vision. I lifted my foot up to trap it dead but missed it completely and it rolled out of play. The crowd started jeering but they didn't realise what was happening to me. At half-time the floodlights came on but it felt like a torch was being flashed in front of my eyes. Minutes later, I could hear the sound of my heart beating like a drum in my ears.

Somehow, I saw the rest of the game out, but as soon as the final whistle blew I left the pitch without shaking hands with the opposition or clapping the away support, and I ran down the tunnel as fast as my weary legs would carry me. I burst inside the dressing room, flung open a cubicle door and started being violently sick and coughing up blood. The lads began filtering in and could hear what was happening. The dressing room fell silent, but for the sound of me vomiting and the tip-tap of studs on the floor. I felt uncomfortable putting them in that position, but what else could I do? Our masseur, Gary Thompson, opened the door and patted me on the back, like I was a drunk with his head buried in the toilet at the end of a heavy night. He urged me to take my time, but said we needed to go and find the doctor and explain what was happening.

I was told it was likely that I had an infection. My immune system had been overwhelmed by cancer and was now struggling to fight off illnesses it would normally combat with ease. I returned to the toilets to continue throwing up. Keith opened the cubicle door. 'You're knocking it on the head,' he said. 'You're done. We need to get you healthy. You've done more than enough for me. Football isn't the be all and end all.

We all love it but you need to get yourself well and healthy for your family.' I nodded my head. It hurt to admit defeat, but he was right. I felt red hot, more so than I normally do after a game, and decided to have a cold shower, but when I came out my temperature was still through the roof. On the coach back, a few of the lads asked me how I was. 'I'm not well,' I said. 'I'm not well at all.' I closed my eyes and drifted in and out of sleep.

A few days later I returned to hospital for another scan, which revealed the tumours had multiplied. I was pencilled in to start my treatment on 3 April. I felt relieved to have a start date at last, but I still had a couple of weeks to kill before it kicked off. Me and Chantelle had always wanted to go on holiday to Thailand and we made an impulsive decision to book flights. I couldn't have the injections I needed to fight off various diseases, like mumps and measles, but after pleading with my doctor, he gave me the green light to go. He knew it could be my last holiday and couldn't bring himself to stand in my way. A few years earlier, we had to cancel a trip to Thailand after Chantelle became pregnant with Lula. In hindsight it was a blessing because she could now come with us and have an amazing life experience at such a young age.

Our plan was to fly to Bangkok and visit various islands dotted around the country. Before we departed, I drafted a statement with Lloydy and gave it to Rochdale to release to the media. I knew that the news would break just as we landed in Thailand. I was literally running away from my problems, but last time I'd felt suffocated by the attention and just wanted space to breathe. Shortly after we arrived, I turned my phone on and my inbox was flooded with messages. I couldn't possibly get back to everyone properly and told them I'd speak to them when I returned. I longed to be free for a couple more weeks, without thinking about what was to come. I was also keen to get a good tan and be as brown as possible to offset the shade of yellow my skin would assume after starting chemo.

You're probably wondering how I managed to relax on holiday, knowing that I had a date with cancer when I returned, but surprisingly I switched off pretty easily. I occupied my thoughts by making sure Lula had the best time possible. Normally when we go away we invite family and friends, but I was happy that on this occasion it was just the three of us because we get along so well together. It's great sharing experiences with other people, but we're a unit and it was amazing to have that one-on-one time, making new memories and opening Lula's eyes to another culture. On the way back we stopped off in Dubai to transfer flights and so Chantelle could buy a new engagement ring, which she'd lost. For the first time I didn't care how much she spent on it. Money becomes so insignificant when your life is in danger.

We were waiting in the departure lounge for our connecting flight when two smiling teenage girls approached us like they had stumbled across a couple of celebrities. 'Are you the couple in the wedding video on Facebook?' asked one of them excitedly. 'Oh my god, you have the perfect family.' We laughed and told them that was indeed us. I found it fascinating that on the outside people thought we were living the perfect life, but they had no idea about the problems we were going through. The power of social media is incredible, but I learnt in that moment more than ever that it only provides the smallest snapshot of your life.

As we drove home from the airport, I glanced in my rear-view mirror and could see Lula scrolling through old pictures on my phone. She stopped and pointed at one with a confused look on her face. 'That's mummy, that's me, but who's that there?' she said. My heart sank and I had to try so hard to stop myself from crying. It was a picture of me during my first fight with cancer. 'That's me Lula,' I said. 'No it's not,' she continued. 'You've got yellow skin and a bald head like a ball.' Chantelle could see I was getting upset but I knew that was the moment I had to tell her. It wasn't how I'd planned it and I didn't want to scare her, but I had to be honest because kids can tell when you're lying. 'That was when daddy was unwell and he's still a bit unwell now,' I said. 'I might have to get some more medicine.' 'You're poorly now?' she said. 'You'd better get to hospital then.' A few days later, that's exactly what I did.

Chapter 15
Ward 15

I COULDN'T feel anything, but I could see and hear the doctor clinking her shiny surgical tools like cutlery, with a mask over her face. The large, plain white bed sheet draped over me had the appearance of a tablecloth ready for a main course, until speckles of blood the colour of red wine began to splatter all over it.

'Are you ok, Joe?' she asked me. 'Yeah, yeah, I'm fine,' I said, unconvincingly. She glanced at my monitor, which showed that my heart was beating faster than when I was running down the wing. 'Don't worry, we're nearly done,' she said. I felt like a slab of meat on a chopping board and, despite my best efforts to shut my eyes and block everything out, I couldn't stop myself from bursting into tears.

I was undergoing a minor operation under local anesthetic to insert a Hickman line into my chest. The first time I'd had cancer, the chemotherapy was delivered into my body via a

PICC line, fed into a vein through my bicep. This was a far more invasive procedure, which required the nurse to make an incision near my collarbone and then tug and pull the tip of a long plastic tube through a vein draining into my heart. The other end tunneled under the skin and came out of another slit in my chest.

Before they began the operation, they showed me a video that explained exactly what would happen and why they were doing it. As well as speeding up the rate at which the chemo entered my bloodstream, it also meant I didn't have to have a needle puncture every time it was administered. The line would remain in place permanently until the end of my treatment. I still have a scar near my collarbone, which I'll have for the rest of my days, but at some point I think I'll get a tattoo to cover it up.

For 45 minutes, I writhed in the bed, praying for it to be all over. The doctor was literally tugging on the line and pulling it through my vein like it was a fishing rod reeling in a fresh carp. It took all my willpower for me to resist grabbing it and pulling it out. Had I done, I would almost certainly have caused myself serious damage and sparked a bloodbath, but luckily I came through it before being wheeled out and parked next to the other guinea pigs undergoing various types of treatment.

Ward 15 became my dressing room. Last time I'd been on a children's ward, but now I was surrounded by grown men of different ages from all walks of life. They didn't know it yet, but in my head they were my team-mates and I felt we'd all have a better chance of survival if we tried to work as a collective. As with all dressing rooms, there are some people you gravitate towards more than others and there were a couple of guys I became close to as we started to talk and help one another through each day.

Karl Benson was a doorman and a big boxing fan, but even his burly frame was struggling to manhandle cancer. By the time I arrived on the ward, he'd already tried six or seven different forms of chemotherapy, all of which had failed to kill the tumours ravaging his body. His doctor had told him he would be taken to a hospital in London to try yet another treatment to see if that would do the trick. He still had hope, but at that stage his outlook was bleak. His energy levels were low and he was really struggling with nausea. Initially, he didn't talk much and would draw the curtains around his bed for much of the day so he could keep himself to himself.

Another of my closest allies was a BBC journalist called Jonathan Ali, who was battling a rare form of leukaemia. He told me that just one in three million people are diagnosed with his type of cancer every year, but somehow he'd fallen victim to it. He was a top guy with a good heart, but at first I didn't know if I could trust him. As a footballer, one of the first rules you learn is to never trust a journalist. I'd decided to switch to a strictly vegan diet and not eat the food supplied by the hospital. It wasn't a case of me turning my nose up at their menu, it was just a choice I'd made which I felt could give me a greater chance of survival. But I feared that Jonathan might hear about it and then twist it into a story. I could already see the headline: 'Footballer rejects NHS food.'

Initially I kept him at arm's length, but I soon realised I was just being paranoid. 'Are we fucked, Joe?' he asked me during one of our many frank discussions. 'We probably look it mate, but I reckon we'll live to fight another day.' He was in his 50s and seemed to know everything, and I enjoyed sitting there and listening to his stories. Luckily for him, he didn't suffer with sickness, so after each bout of chemo, he'd take himself off downstairs to the hospital canteen and treat himself to his favourite breakfast. Every time he returned, I'd ask him what he'd eaten and the answer was always the same. 'I was going to have something healthy, but I thought sod it, I'm having sausage and eggs. You can stick to your rabbit food, Joe.' He liked to give me a bit of stick but I knew he was a softie really. He lived in a house next door to his mum, so she was on hand to look after him when he went home.

I began to think about the dressing rooms that I'd been in and what makes a good one. There is no set formula but you have to have a good variety of characters. Firstly, you need leaders, people who will set the tone with their professionalism and speak on behalf of the group. You also need jokers, who can put a positive spin on any situation and defuse negativity. Quiet types can offer a different perspective because they see things in a clearer state of mind. Then you need the no-nonsense sorts who have a bit of fire in their belly and won't stand for any bullshit. If you're feeling sorry for yourself or you're getting the shit kicked out of you on the pitch, you want these guys in the trenches with you.

We're all built differently, and having the emotional intelligence to respect that is really important. When I was at Bury, Gary Neville came in and did a talk. He told us a story about when he used to room with David Beckham on away trips. They were good mates from the youth team and sharing a room the night before a game really helped them to bond on and off the pitch. But when Becks started seeing Victoria, he would call her in the early hours of the morning while she was away on a tour in Asia or Australia. Neville spoke to Fergie and said he needed to room with someone else because he had a very strict routine. He would be in bed at 9pm and get up at 5am. Becks' routine wasn't in sync with his own, so he needed to be with someone who was a better fit.

I could relate to that anecdote inside the hospital but also in the Rochdale dressing room. My room-mate on away trips was Calvin Andrew. He's the most positive person I've ever met in my life. It doesn't matter if he's been smashed to pieces by a defender or had a bad game, he just brushes it off. He's kept me going if I've been sat on the bench. He always says, 'Keep your head up and keep going.' We have similar music tastes and we can talk about anything and everything. He's travelled the world and has played and been in and around Premier League dressing rooms. He's got some great stories, which I love listening to. He's also a chameleon in social situations and can assess a mood in a camp. If he's in a room with certain people he knows how to change and be more serious. For me he's been a breath of fresh air. I'm a positive person, but not every day. If there's something wrong with me then people around me will know about it and keep their distance for a little while.

We had some deep conversations on that ward, but we were still able to have a laugh, which helped to raise spirits in the camp when one of us was having a rough day. Still, there were constant reminders of the severity of our situation. There was a young lad in the bed opposite me who could only have been about 21, but he looked like death. He'd basically been told that the treatment hadn't worked and he now had to choose whether to stay in hospital for end of life care or go home and see out his final days. I wanted to put my fingers in my ears and block out what I'd just heard. I wouldn't wish witnessing that conversation on my worst enemy. 'Why the fuck is this happening to him?' I thought. I dread to think what was going through his head at that moment. His life had barely started. There were memories he'd never make, places he'd never see and loved ones he'd have to leave behind.

'Stop!' The voice in my head interrupted my internal monologue and ordered me to pull the shutters down. Working myself up over someone else's heartache wasn't going to make me feel any better. I made a silent vow to myself that I wouldn't end up having the same conversation with my doctor. Maybe I'd been naive investing so much energy into other people's battles. Sure, we were a team, but we were all here to save ourselves, nobody else. In a dressing room you have to be there for your team-mates when things aren't going well but first and foremost you need to make sure you've got your own house in order. I looked around the room and knew that everyone else was thinking the same thing. Some of them would rarely speak because all they wanted was to focus on themselves. I couldn't cut myself off to that extent because mentally I don't think it's healthy, but I had to be selfish and work out my own gameplan.

The chemo was relentless. Each cycle lasted 24 hours and I had just 20 minutes between each one to get a shower or something to eat before I had to be back in bed and hooked up to the machines. This would continue for six days, after which I was allowed to go home for a week, providing I was well enough, before returning for more. I had no pattern to my days. At night, the nurses would turn the lights off at about 11pm. Some of the blokes would go to sleep, while others would pull their curtains shut, turn on their bedside lamp and read or watch a film with their headphones in. I was a night owl and the nurse on the night shift would always be shocked to see that I was still awake in the early hours of the morning. It made me laugh how they would creep into the ward to check our machines were working and wear headlamps like SAS soldiers on a top-secret mission, so that they didn't wake up the other patients.

Christie Hospital is only about 20 minutes away from Rochdale's training ground, so I had a steady stream of visitors to keep my spirits up. One of the lads who pulled up a chair by my bedside was Nathaniel Mendez-Laing. He's three years younger than me and had only been at the club just over 12 months, but we had a lot in common. He was born in Birmingham and, like me, had quite a tough childhood, but football stopped him from going down the wrong path. His troubles had given him a streetwise confidence that you need in a football dressing room. At the start of the season, he found himself on the bench because I'd taken his place in the starting line-up. One afternoon, Keith put two teams up on a whiteboard; one was the first team and the other was the second string. Once again, he was playing second fiddle.

'Don't be thinking you're going to be in that starting line-up for long,' he said to me. I couldn't believe he had the confidence to lay down that sort of challenge in front of the other lads. 'Listen, you're going to have to do something special to get this shirt off me,' I replied. As shocked as I was, I respected his mindset. You don't see enough of that in football dressing rooms because players are afraid to rock the boat and don't want to be seen as a bad apple. But ultimately, you're all individuals in a team sport. Nobody wants to be sat on the bench every week. You want to be on the pitch, scoring goals, making assists and receiving the plaudits for helping your team get three points. That sounds like a selfish mentality, but achieving your personal goals will benefit the team and push the immediate competition in your position to play better.

That bit of tension between us made us closer. While I was in hospital, he took his chance in the first team and scored some brilliant goals. When he came to see me, the day before a game against Gillingham, he promised me he was going to score a goal and dedicate it to me. I told him not to put that sort of pressure on himself, but what did he go and do? That's right, he scored. He celebrated by running to the bench, where they had a shirt with my name on the back and lifting it in the air.

That was a really special moment, knowing that the dressing room hadn't forgotten about me. It was also great to see Nathaniel fulfilling his potential, even though he was doing it in my position. He'd had a few run-ins with Keith over various things but had settled down now he was playing on a regular basis. At the end of that season he moved on to Cardiff and then got promoted to the Premier League last season. It's amazing what can happen when the penny finally drops. I'm just glad I don't have to fight him for my shirt anymore.

You never really know how much people think of you until you're seriously ill, or at least I never did. I was amazed that two of my team-mates, Keith Keane and Andy Cannon, came to visit me. We got along perfectly well, but we weren't best mates or anything like that. Still, they wanted to see how I was and offer their support. I was also moved by my mate Dan Handford, who drove all the way from Carlisle just a few weeks after his wife gave birth to their second child.

We first met when he was a youth-team player at Rochdale and used to clean my boots. Our paths crossed again when I moved to Carlisle and we became good friends. Like several goalkeepers I've played with, he's got a bit of a screw loose. He thought nothing of jumping in his car and driving two hours down the motorway with his newborn baby in the passenger seat just to come and sit with me for a couple of hours. My best mate, James Rothwell, was another regular visitor, as was my former Tranmere team-mate Max Power.

At the end of my first week of chemo, my doctor told me I would have a three-week break before my next cycle. I'd felt better, but the full side effects hadn't yet kicked in, so me and Chantelle booked flights to Spain. If I had a bad turn then we could get a flight home and be back within a few hours. Our plan was to land in Alicante and then hire a car and drive up to Barcelona, stopping off at various places along the way. Lula was in school but we persuaded her teachers to let us break the rules a little bit and take her with us, but we kept it a secret from her.

When we picked her up, we told her we were going to the David Lloyd leisure centre, which she loves because they have a big outdoor pool. 'We're going the wrong way,' she said, as we drove towards the airport. 'No, no, we're just taking another road,' I replied. When we got there, I opened the boot with our cases in. 'We're going on holiday,' I said. 'You're lying, I've school tomorrow,' she said. She only believed me once I got her passport out and we started walking through the airport. That must've been amazing for her. One minute she'd been in school, probably getting a bit bored in class, the next minute she was on a plane to Spain, still wearing her school uniform.

We stayed in a beautiful hotel with a pool, which was bathed in sunshine, but I couldn't have a dip in case I got dirt in my Hickman line. Normally you're supposed to get it cleaned every three days, but I'd convinced my doctor it would be fine if we waited a bit longer. I ended up having some really good conversations with the other holidaymakers by the pool, who seemed to be drawn to me because I was just relaxing on my own in the shade wearing a t-shirt.

One morning, I was waiting for the lift when a 6ft 6in Norwegian guy came up to me. He looked like a Viking. I'd been watching a series set during that period and he would've been a perfect fit. The first thing he did was glance at my crucifix. 'Do you believe in God?' he asked me. I was a bit taken aback by his line of questioning. 'Erm ... yeah, I think there's someone out there,' I said. 'I saw you by the pool yesterday, why didn't you jump in? You've got lovely brown skin,' he continued. For some reason I felt comfortable enough to explain my situation to him. 'You are a child of God,' he said. 'Keep believing and walking forward and your life will turn around.'

We got out of the lift but before I had the chance to say goodbye he'd vanished. I couldn't believe that a giant of a man had disappeared into thin air. I had some breakfast and then went to find Chantelle and tell her about the conversation I'd just had. I was halfway through my story when my phone started ringing. 'No caller ID' flashed on my screen. Whenever I see that I know it's the hospital, so I answered it immediately.

Dr Gibbs was on the other end of the line. He told me my scan results had returned and though I still had tumours in my body, the cancer had turned off and wasn't growing. I would still have to continue chemo, but it was positive news. I was heading in the right direction. Chantelle could see my reaction and came over to find out what was going on. I explained what he'd said and she was elated. We decided to prolong our holiday for another few days. It was against doctor's orders but we'd just had some good luck so thought we'd keep rolling the dice.

Our next stop was Salou, where I had a feeling of déjà vu. I went there on my first foreign holiday when I was nine years old with my dad and his girlfriend at the time. I remember it broke my mum's heart. She couldn't afford to take us away anywhere in England, never mind Spain, and she knew dad had funded the trip through illegal means. Returning was like stamping a tattoo over an old wound. Lula had the time of her life and before we headed back we spent a couple of days in Valencia to round off the trip. The combination of sunshine, good news and the company of my two girls did wonders for my morale.

When I returned for my next round of chemo the following week, I felt like my batteries were well and truly recharged. It turned out they needed to be because I was about to experience the scariest day of my life. After pulling through another six days of intensive chemo, I returned home, but suddenly everything went horribly wrong. I was used to being sick, but in the space of three hours I vomited 60 to 70 times. It started off as sick, then water, followed by cola-coloured bile. There was nothing left inside me but my innards, but I still couldn't stop retching, while my temperature continued to soar.

Chantelle pressed the emergency red button on my personal alarm and an ambulance arrived within minutes. Two paramedics came into the house and found me lying down on the floor in my bedroom. They helped me to my feet and then slowly ushered me into the back of the ambulance and took me back to hospital. The first 100 yards of the journey was torture. Our house is on a long, cobbled road, so I was wobbling from side to side like I was on a roller coaster. The paramedic threw special salts into my bowl so the sick solidified quickly and didn't splash back into my face, but still I continued to vomit.

I was so scared. People can die from chemotherapy and I thought I was going to have a heart attack or one of my major organs was about to fail. Chantelle is a strong woman but I could see the fear in her face. When I arrived at the hospital they put me on a drip for 24 hours to replace the fluids I'd lost and thankfully my sickness began to subside. It was a huge blow to the momentum I'd built up and the guy in the bed next to me dented my mood even more. He kept moaning about the food he'd been given and later told me that he was going to die. I felt for him, I really did, but I'd managed to shield myself from negativity and hearing his plight really messed with my head. I became short-tempered and snappy with people. I felt like I'd gone one-nil in front but had been pegged back.

After each cycle of chemo, I became progressively weaker. Every day a nurse would come round and ask me to fill in a questionnaire. It was a series of simple questions, asking me if I could still use the TV remote, brush my own teeth or get out of bed without help. At first I thought they were daft, but I began to understand why they needed answers as even the most basic of tasks became difficult. I began to suffer terrible vein pain in my wrists and at one point I couldn't fasten the buttons on my shirt because my hands were hurting so much. It felt like that throbbing feeling you get when you've been out in the cold in the middle of winter without gloves on and then put your hands in hot water, but ten times worse.

I was determined to remain as independent as possible even when a fire broke out at the hospital. I looked out of the window and could see the flames and smoke from my bed. Workers had been carrying out welding work on the roof of the Paterson building, but hot debris had fallen off and landed on cardboard and fabric below, sparking the blaze and causing millions of pounds worth of damage. Research papers had gone up in smoke and hordes of patients had been evacuated. The nurses warned us that if it continued to spread then we would be taken out via a lift. I told them that if it did I would leave of my own accord and sprint down the stairs.

I still had plenty of fire in my belly, but I could tell the flame had gone out in the eyes of some of the other patients. There was one guy who was waiting to be taken home in an ambulance. He'd been made redundant, he had no wife, no kids and no support apart from the doctors and nurses treating him. He won't be alive now, no chance. Cancer hurts, but fighting it alone must crush your spirit beyond repair. The pain can only go on for so long and it only ends one of two ways. You hope it stops because you're cured, but not everyone is so lucky. If you're in constant pain every day then there must be a point when you just want to be put out of your misery.

I was lucky to have different teams fighting my corner. I had doctors and nurses with years of experience in their field behind me and a close-knit family unit who lived round the corner to keep me company. I also had my team-mates on hand for moral support. And of course, I had my boys on the ward, who were the only ones who truly understood what I was going through. Collectively, I had a squad of people who I could draw energy from, but nothing they said could prepare me for what would happen next.

After my last round of chemo, I would have to undergo a stem cell transplant, which meant I could face up to two months in an isolation unit. It was essential to give my immune system the chance to repair itself away from the outside world and deal with the worst of the side effects, which were about to unleash hell on my body. If I came into contact with germs, it could prove fatal because I only had a small number of white blood cells to fight them. The prospect of spending that length of time in my own company, away from Chantelle and Lula, filled me with dread. I was given a couple of days to go home and gather my thoughts before beginning the toughest battle of my life. I packed up my things and readied myself for war.

Chapter 16
18 days

THE room was a blank canvas, filled with the stench of bleach. All I had for company was a television, an en suite and a lonely window, which offered me the only glimpse of the outside world I would have for up to two months. I'd overcome battles at home, in the playground and on the football pitch, but this was different, this was life or death, and my opponent was hell-bent on getting revenge.

It was 3 June 2017, and I was sat on my bed in one of the dozens of isolation rooms at Christie Hospital, preparing for my final week of chemo, before undergoing a stem cell transplant. The chemo was that powerful, it had attacked cancerous cells, but also killed white and red blood cells and platelets I needed to fight infections, transport oxygen around my body and basically stay alive. This meant I had to be locked away for an indefinite period of time until my immune system was strong enough to survive in the outside world without medical assistance.

Before my treatment, my doctor had removed thousands of healthy cells from my body, which had been stored in a freezer, and would now be fed back into my system via a drip inserted into a vein over a period of four to five hours. If everything went to plan, they would slowly begin to grow and multiply in the weeks ahead until I was healthy enough to leave isolation. My time alone would also give me the privacy to deal with the worst side effects of chemo, which were about to hit me like a tsunami.

Players are often perceived as alpha males, devoid of emotion, and trained to bottle up their fears as a way of surviving in a ruthless sport. That might be true for some, but I've never seen myself as a macho man, and would openly admit I was scared of what lay ahead. However, I'm certain I'm mentally stronger than 99 per cent of the people I come up against because of the things I've been through. I was convinced that would give me an edge, because this was a test that would challenge my mind as well as my body.

When my doctor came in to explain the process, I asked him not to tell me which symptoms I was likely to experience and make sure the nurses did the same. It was my way of waging mental warfare against cancer – if I knew exactly what was coming, then perhaps my mind would begin playing tricks on me and I'd imagine pain that wasn't really there. Instead, I wanted to know the record time a patient had recovered from a stem cell transplant and made it out of isolation. His answer was 21 days.

Footballers relish having targets to hit and in my head I vowed to break that barrier.

The night before a match I often visualise certain situations I think I'll encounter so I'm mentally and physically primed for every possible scenario. Although I didn't know specifically what I was about to endure, in my head I went through the same process of imagining how my body might break down and waste away over the days and weeks ahead. I imagined I'd be like a drug addict, shivering and sweating, after trying to go cold turkey following years of abuse. It turned out my imagination had painted an accurate picture of what would be the loneliest weeks of my life.

I'd been in isolation for 72 hours when my mobile phone began to ring. I instantly recognised it was a prison phone number. It was my dad. Our relationship had been pretty much non-existent since I moved to Manchester when I was eight, but he'd found out about my plight from a relative. 'We're in the same boat now Joe, we're both locked away,' he said.

His words angered me; I was in this situation through no fault of my own, but he was behind bars because he'd repeatedly broken the law. I put him in his place and he apologised immediately. The conversation was over in a matter of minutes but I told him that once, or if, I got back on both feet, I wanted to see him face to face to get answers to the questions that had rattled around my head since I was a little boy. He said he was going nowhere fast and promised he'd tell me everything I wanted to know.

Isolation gives you a rare opportunity to reflect away from the constant distractions of daily life. I wondered how my dad could sleep at night knowing he'd missed out on so many important moments in mine and Reuben's lives, as well as the other kids he'd fathered over the years, purely because of the selfish mistakes he'd made. At some point he must've been haunted by his actions. Part of me feels sorry for him; at his age he should be a proud granddad, reflecting on a successful life. Instead, he's just another number in a prison cell, living with the dead weight of regret hanging round his neck. In a way, that is a bigger punishment than a prison sentence.

I don't know whether it was a side effect of the treatment or because I had so much time on my hands to think, but I also started to feel paranoid about the motives of some of the people who had come to see me. A few I'd class more as acquaintances than friends had asked if they could take a selfie while I was in bed looking like death. It made me feel uncomfortable – I wanted them to visit me because they cared, not to show the world that they'd done a good deed so they could get a few likes on Instagram or Facebook. Perhaps I was thinking too much into it, but I do find it strange how the world has changed, nothing seems to be private anymore.

To pass the time, I'd spend hours scrolling through my phone looking at old pictures and videos and seeing what my friends were up to on Snapchat and Instagram. In hindsight, it wasn't a wise decision. I saw team-mates on holiday in Las Vegas with smiles on their faces. I'd been there 12 months ago for my stag do and had the time of my life with my closest friends. I wondered if I'd had my last holiday, but I tried to combat those negative thoughts by reminding myself of the rich life I'd lived up until that point. I'd played football for a living, married the girl of my dreams and recreated life. If this was the end of the road, I was content with everything I'd achieved at 28.

I'd been in isolation for seven days when the side effects began to surface. My concentration started to waver and I became increasingly sensitive to light, which meant watching DVDs and reading books was almost impossible. Up until that point, I'd been able to eat and drink as normal, but now I was struggling to keep food and liquid down again and slowly my weight began to plummet. More worryingly, I noticed a change in my doctor's tone of voice and the nurses who cared for me on a daily basis. They sounded panicked as their visits became more frequent and they continually asked me whether I was feeling ok.

I needed blood transfusions to try and boost my white and red blood cell count, but my body couldn't rely on them forever. I began to wonder if I'd underestimated the suffering I was about to endure. Prior to the treatment, I'd been dismissive when the doctor had warned me that one patient had spent two and a half months in isolation. I dread to think the state he must have been in. Physically and mentally, he would've been nothing more than an empty shell by the time he left.

If I felt well enough, I was allowed to leave my room and sit in a hub at the end of a corridor, where I could chat with other people undergoing the same treatment and briefly escape the prison of my mind. But I made a conscious decision not to. There were 40 other rooms at the hospital and I knew we wouldn't all make it out alive. My room was my war cabin. Not all of us were going to survive, so I stayed in there, curled up in the foetal position, and entered survival mode. I could feel myself gradually getting weaker. My gut started playing up and I constantly had to use a bedpan, which made me feel like an old man. I needed help from the nurses just to use the toilet – I felt vulnerable and embarrassed.

On day ten, hallucinations haunted me throughout the day and night. During one bizarre episode, I was convinced a SWAT team had abseiled down the outside wall of my room, smashed my windows in and were about to perform open-heart surgery while I was strapped to the bed fully conscious. I woke up shivering and sweating like Gollum in the corner of the room with a nurse looking over me. 'Everything is ok Joe, you're going to be fine, you've just had a bad dream,' she said softly. My mind was so scrambled I had to ask her several days later whether the incident had been a figment of my imagination. Apparently it's a common by-product of powerful chemo, but I still felt embarrassed, a bit like when you're reminded of something you did or said after a few drinks on a night out.

Emotionally, the following three days were by some distance the worst of my life, as I became consumed by depression. I spent 36 hours in and out of sleep. Every time I woke up my bed looked as if a dog had shed its fur over the sheets and pillows. The hair on my head, in my nostrils and even my ears had been shed. I desperately missed my daughter. It was the longest period we'd been apart since she had been born and I worried what impact my suffering would have on her in the future.

She'd only recently lost her granddad, Chantelle's father, to lung cancer and she'd often wake up in the night crying because she missed him. I think the first four years of a child's life are so important and I wondered whether the whole episode would affect her emotional development. I also felt gutted for my mum. The son she had created and brought up was crumbling into a bag of bones. Reuben was away in San Francisco on business for two weeks so he wasn't around to offer her the emotional support he often gives her during unstable times.

My white blood cell count remained dangerously low and I desperately needed my levels to shoot up. I'd lost nearly two stone in weight and was encouraged to try drinking protein shakes and eating eggs to get my weight up. I went against doctor's orders, having chosen to follow a vegan diet. Something had caused the disease to come back again and I wanted to make sure I did everything in my power to ensure it would never return. Chantelle made me plant-based meals and brought them to the hospital every day, despite the fact I was still struggling to keep them down. I had also decided to completely cut out processed sugars. When I underwent a PET scan, prior to my diagnosis, I was told that cancerous cells feed off glucose. There was no chance I was going to eat or drink anything that could potentially allow them to grow.

After three days of horrendous suffering, my white blood cell count at last began to shoot up, which meant the stem cell transplant was working. My first wedding anniversary was approaching and I was deemed well enough for Chantelle to pay me a brief visit to celebrate. Before she arrived at the hospital, I watched our wedding video back on my iPad. It brought a tear to my eye as I relived the happiest day of our lives.

She knows I love buying trainers and so she bought me a pair I'd wanted for a long time, along with a large balloon. I felt terrible that I couldn't give her anything in return, but we made the best of a bad situation. She joined me in my single bed and we curled up and watched *Love Island* on TV like two teenagers. I watched contestants on the show declaring their love for people they had known for a matter of weeks. My wife had remained by my side in sickness and health – that's true love.

There was still one other little person I was desperate to see. Children are normally banned from visiting under any circumstances, but with Father's Day just around the corner, I decided to defy doctor's orders and asked Chantelle to bring Lula in.

She'd only recently recovered from chicken pox, but I was confident I could shake off any bugs she'd potentially pass on. The nurses warned me of the risks of contracting an infection, but my mind was made up, because I knew she would give me a real emotional boost.

I hadn't washed in two days, because the change in temperature when I stepped into the shower cubicle caused me to be sick, but I made a special effort for my little girl because I didn't want her to be alarmed when she saw me. It had been nearly two weeks since I'd seen her, but I could already notice minute changes in her appearance. She was only with me for about 40 minutes or so and spent most of it playing games on my iPad, but it was worth it just to receive a card she'd made for me and to see her smile after I gave her a hug. In that moment, I fully understood what Paul had said about being energised by Lula. I felt like I'd been plugged into the mains and given a boost of power.

My spirits had been raised and I could feel my competitive streak beginning to return. I was still in the game. I hadn't forgotten about my 21-day target and as my health continued to improve, so too did my belief that I could beat that record. I found I could boost my motivation by drawing up a list of targets I wanted to achieve and changes I'd make to my life once I was out.

My list started with small goals, such as climbing the stairs, reading Lula a bedtime story and putting on a certain amount of weight. I also had medium-term targets, like running again and kicking a ball, all leading up to the long-term goal of returning to football at the level I'd left. I also promised myself that I would never surround myself with negative people once I was out. If you walk around with a cloud over your head, it's going to rain.

On day 16, my friend Nicky Adams and Rochdale team-mate Brian Barry-Murphy joined Chantelle by my bedside. Shortly after they arrived, Dr Gibbs came in with some news. 'You'll be glad to hear your immune system is strong enough for you to go home, Joe.' My reaction should have been one of pure elation, but instead it was mixed with fear. I held on tightly to the metal rails on the side of my bed and argued that it was too soon. I realised I'd almost become institutionalised. I was used to having nurses on hand to give me injections and a big red button I could press in the event I had a bad turn. I was scared of going back out into the big bad world and worried my immune system wouldn't be strong enough to cope. I looked at Nicky and asked him not to tell anyone about my reaction. I was embarrassed and didn't want people to think I'd gone soft while I was inside.

The hospital never gives patients a set day and time to leave because they know that while many are physically ready to go, emotionally they are still unstable and need time to prepare themselves for life outside of the white box which has become their home. In the end it didn't take me long to pull myself together. I told Chantelle to pick Lula up from school and bring her into the hospital for 1pm the following day. The three of us would leave together as a family.

It was an amazing day, with loads of friends, including a few of the lads from my stag do, coming in to help me pack my bags. My physio at Bury, Nick Meace, made a mammoth journey from Portsmouth to see me and gave me a wonderful gift with all our family photos in it, which him and his girlfriend, Francesca, had put together.

As I left the room for the first time in 18 days, I realised I'd smashed my target and set a new record for an isolation patient at Christie Hospital. My doctor was amazed. The only obstacle left in my path was the exit doors. I held on to Lula's hand and held a balloon Chan had brought in to celebrate our first wedding anniversary a few days earlier. I reached the reception area and thanked all the nurses for everything they had done for me and the lady who had asked me every day if I wanted food, even though I declined every time because I just couldn't keep it down.

As I walked through the exit door, tears began to roll down my face and my nose started to run. I hadn't felt wind on my skin in over two weeks and had no nostril hairs to stop the fresh air from rushing into my head. I walked slowly down a ramp towards the car park but stopped after feeling a sharp pain in my calf. I was convinced I'd torn it as I stepped down on to flat ground. My muscles were so weak and couldn't cope with the simplest of movements. We packed my suitcases into the car and then I sat in the front passenger seat ready to go home. Before we set off, I asked Chantelle to take it easy on the roads because I was so frail. I could literally feel every bump and turn in the road like a crash dummy in one of those car adverts.

The sun was still shining brightly when we got home, so I pulled up a chair in the back garden and basked in the warm feeling of the rays hitting my skin. I'd been told I'd still need to return to the hospital to receive injections to bolster my immune system for several weeks, but I was out of the woods. The chemotherapy and stem cell transplant had been a success and somehow I'd beaten cancer for a second time. But it wasn't enough just to survive.

Chapter 17

The comeback kid

I LOOKED in the mirror and saw a 16-year-old boy staring back at me. He wasn't wearing cubic zirconia earrings or combing his afro. In fact, he didn't have any hair at all. His skin had a yellow tint and was wrapped tightly around a face that was weathered beyond its years. His alien body didn't look like it belonged to this earth, either, with every bone jutting out like a Halloween skeleton.

I was stood in my bedroom naked but I didn't recognise myself. I hadn't weighed ten stone since I was a first-year YTS at Rochdale. It was the morning after I'd arrived home and the first time I'd seen the full impact chemotherapy had had on my body. I wasn't a pretty sight. My closest friends and family recognised me, but if you were an acquaintance you would have needed a second look to realise it was me.

I felt like I'd been stripped of my identity and sent back in time. I had a wife and a child but physically I was 16 again. I could fall asleep at any moment, just like I used to when

I came home from training when I was going through my growth spurt. Back then, I'd developed a love for trainers and my first step towards regaining my identity was to put on the pair Chantelle had bought me for our wedding anniversary, even though I knew they couldn't carry me very far.

The first physical target I'd been set by my doctor was to try and walk 100 yards outside. The athlete inside me sniggered at the distance, but I wasn't laughing as I hobbled down the road like an old man, carefully putting one foot in front of the other to stop myself from losing my balance and falling over. I was exhausted and felt like I'd run a cross-country race. I had a pensioner's engine inside a teenager's body. I was out of hospital but still struggling to stand on my own two feet. Blackouts were a frequent occurrence and I'd often open my eyes with no idea how I'd ended up on the floor.

I craved my independence and wanted to jump in the car, put my foot down and drive somewhere far away with my tunes on, but I still wasn't allowed in case I fell asleep at the wheel. Chantelle was my chauffeur, as well as my carer, and drove us both to the Lake District for a short break about a week after I'd returned home. We'd been invited by Phil Ercolano, the owner of Cassius Camps and the man who had beasted me while I was on trial with Carlisle. He'd paid for us to stay at a beautiful hotel called The Lakeside, not far from the camp, and as part of the deal I'd agreed to drop by and talk to Sheffield Wednesday's under-23 team about my story.

Later that evening, I returned to the dining hall where we'd started our camp two years ago. I'd done my research on the team and knew there were a few talented lads in there who had represented their country at youth-team level and were on the brink of first-team football. It's a challenging period in a player's career, particularly in the modern game. Some make the mistake of thinking they've already made it. They're earning half-decent money and their Instagram accounts imitate a player's lifestyle. But before they know it they've slipped down the divisions and never realised their potential. I wanted them to understand the setbacks that would inevitably come along the way and the resilience they needed and would be built at the camp.

As I walked slowly to the front of the room I could tell they were shocked by my appearance, but it was the perfect way to grab their attention. I spoke for over half an hour about my journey and how it had led to this moment. By the end I was exhausted and asked for a chair to sit down on while I fielded questions from the boys. It was another character-building experience. Before I started talking, my legs were shaking and my mouth was dry like I was stepping up to take a penalty in a shootout. Players in team sports aren't used to being in individual situations where all the attention is on them. Usually you're surrounded by your team-mates and opponents but I didn't have anyone to take the heat off me or play a little five-yard pass to. A few of the boys asked for pictures at the end before I wished them good luck for the following day; they were going to need it.

A week later a mate of mine, James Poole, who works in the scouting department at Manchester City, asked me to do another talk with their academy boys. I agreed to it but was left stunned when a voice called my name from one of the rooms inside an office at the training ground. It was Pep Guardiola. I've met David Beckham, Paul Scholes and the Neville brothers and never once been star-struck, but for the next five minutes I acted like a little girl, laughing nervously and agreeing with everything he said. He told me I was welcome to use the club's facilities for my rehabilitation and only needed to ask if I wanted to attend a game once the season had started. It was an incredible gesture and I couldn't believe he even knew my name. His attention to detail reminded me of when I crossed paths with Fergie when I was a kid. He liked to have control of everything and was aware of every single person who entered that training ground. My only regret is that I didn't ask him more questions in the time I spent with him.

The City lads were a different bunch to those at Sheffield Wednesday. They had everything at their disposal. If they wanted to get stronger, there were four or five strength and conditioning coaches on hand to design programmes tailored specifically for their needs. If they wanted to hone their finishing after training, there were mannequins everywhere and numerous perfectly manicured pitches to choose from. The club were wary of them becoming spoilt and taking everything for granted, which is why they'd asked me to come in. I focused my talk on my fall from grace after leaving Manchester United and my grounding experiences on trial at various clubs lower down the leagues. I wanted them to know it could easily be them if things didn't work out at City or they failed to put in the hard yards.

It felt liberating telling people about my story, but it still didn't have the ending I wanted. A month after leaving hospital, I returned to Rochdale to meet the manager and the boys and start planning my route back to first-team football. They definitely weren't expecting a bag of bones to walk through the door and I could see the shock on their faces. Beechy immediately laid down a challenge. 'I want ten goals from you this season,' he said. 'Let's get you back for January.' My doctor would've had a heart attack if he'd heard the conversation. Patients with normal office jobs are advised to start easing back into work over a period of 12 months. They were expecting me to do the same thing in training, but I only had another season left on my contract and didn't have time to waste.

My rehab was like putting a broken car back together. I started off with a basic MOT, which involved testing every single muscle to see which ones were working properly and those that were going to need a bit of oil to get them going again. My first session was a ten-minute walk on a treadmill followed by a few stretches and a rub-down from the masseur. Just like last time, he couldn't believe how lumpy and full of fluid my legs were. We then progressed to basic movements in the gym, to see how I felt when I did exercises like squats or bicep curls. I was so weak it was a joke. If someone had called me a youth-team player for a laugh I'd have flipped because I was so self-conscious about my lack of strength. I'd put in a lot of work over the years to get fitter and stronger, so it was soul-destroying to be back at square one.

My immune system was still weak so I couldn't spend long around the other lads in case I picked up an infection, and I used hand sanitisers to keep any germs at bay. Still, that didn't stop them from putting their head around the physio's door and asking me if I was having another day off. Keith's wit was also ruthless. 'Here he is, the cheerleader, where are your pom-poms?' he said, prompting howls of laughter from the lads. I laughed it off and then decided to wind him up by lifting tiny pink dumb-bells in the gym. He bit every time. They're a harsh bunch, but being back amongst the dressing room banter did wonders for my morale. Keith also knew that his little digs would motivate me to try and shove his words down his throat, so it was great man-management.

After three or four weeks I had a good feel for what my body was capable of, but when I attempted to up the intensity and do a 2km run on the treadmill the pain nearly reduced me to tears. My body was like a car running low on oil, with black smoke coming out of the bonnet. My lungs were burning and my legs were heavy, like they'd been tied down with bricks. Our strength and conditioning coach, Kevin Higgins, could see I was struggling and came over and stopped the machine. I hobbled off and held back the tears. The realisation of the size of the task ahead had come crashing down on me. We finished the session early and I went home to lick my wounds, but there was no chance I was going to give up. I was going to have to dust myself down, bite down hard on my gumshield and grind my way back.

Every morning, Kevin rang me up to see how my body was feeling and if I was coming in. I always did. Even if I just had a stretch or a rub-down, it felt like progress. I loved working one-on-one with him. He was a third-year youth-team player at Rochdale when I joined, before being released. I was petrified of him when I was younger and I'm still scared of him now because his sessions are always intense. Every evening, he'd send me my data so I could see how hard I'd worked and that I was improving. It helped working with someone who knew my personality but also how a player's mind works. He knew how to put together a session that would keep me mentally stimulated and set small achievable targets to boost my morale. Keith would often ask why I was only doing a light session, but he never succumbed to pressure and always made sure we did things step by step.

It was all well and good me running in straight lines on a treadmill, but I knew the real challenge would be getting back out on the grass and changing direction. The first time I put my boots back on I could feel every stud through my soles. You don't realise that your feet must harden through years of playing football every day. We started off with basic 20m or 30m runs to see how my body coped with the resistance of pushing off on grass, followed by passing drills over various distances. I couldn't believe how weak my legs were. I couldn't manage more than two or three long-range passes over 30 or 40 yards before the ball was coming back towards me in the wind. I just had to laugh. I felt like I was a little kid again trying to kick a size five ball for the first time.

One of my biggest challenges was performing repeated sprints with little rest in between each one. My recovery was just too slow between the runs, so I'd still be knackered by the time I started the next one. Aside from having done no running for about six months, my red blood cell count still wasn't optimal, which meant there was less oxygen being pumped around my body. My other problem was trying to put the weight back on that I'd lost. My vegan diet meant the progress was slower than if I'd been eating meat, but I felt I'd be leaner and healthier in the long run with my new approach. Keith found it hard to get his head around it. 'You're a man, you need red meat Joe,' he said. 'Get yourself to McDonald's and get a few burgers down your neck.' He was only half-joking and kept asking me how much I weighed. I knew he wouldn't allow me to train with the rest of the lads until I hit a certain number and he was confident I had the physique to handle myself in tackles.

If you're not familiar with a vegan diet, it's pretty simple. It involves eating an entirely plant-based diet, and cutting out foods that come from animals, like meat, dairy and eggs. I decided to become vegan after speaking to a dietician and doing some research on the various causes of cancer. Eating meat puts your body into an acidic state, which is the perfect environment for cancerous cells to multiply. I also binned protein shakes. I'm not saying they're bad for you, but casein, which is in a lot of supplements, is like rocket fuel for cancer, so I just had to get rid of them. I was worried about where I would get my protein from to recover efficiently between games but learned I could get more than enough from various types of beans and natural protein supplements. Luckily, I have a friend called Dean Howells, who runs his own company called Rev Foods. I called him every night to ask him what he and his wife were cooking so I could learn new recipes. It's easy to get enough calories and protein from other sources, it's just a case of re-educating yourself.

As my hair started to grow back, I felt it was thicker and blacker than it had been before. I also noticed the purple rings on my fingernails, which are a by-product of chemotherapy, disappeared a lot faster than after my first treatment four years ago, which I attribute to my diet. I also have blood test results from my doctors, one after eating a normal diet containing dairy, meat and some processed sugars, and another after eating a vegan diet. There is a big difference between the two, in favour of my new diet. The staff were amazed by the effect nutrition had had on my body's performance. It might not be for everyone, but for me it has been a game changer.

It took six hard months of training before I was ready to make my return. I was nowhere near fit enough to play for 90 minutes, but I knew I had enough in the tank to make an impact off the bench and that my game understanding would get me through it. Keith included me in his squad for our home game against Walsall, two days before Christmas. Ironically, the fixture was one day short of a year since I'd been diagnosed with cancer for a second time. Chantelle, mum, Reuben and my mentor, Martin Robert Hall, were in the crowd when I came on as a substitute with 18 minutes to go. It was a moment I'll never forget and I could've cried as I ran on to the pitch. I received an incredible reception from the crowd, which gave me goosebumps. To cross the white line again felt so rewarding and I very nearly wrote the perfect comeback story. With just a few minutes remaining, the ball fell to me inside the penalty area and I drilled it towards goal. My old Carlisle team-mate, Mark Gillespie, was in goal, but was helpless as it flew past him, only for a defender to stop it on the goal line and somehow scramble it clear. I protested with the referee and claimed it had crossed the line but he was having none of it. I was convinced that was my moment, but it wasn't to be. The main thing was that I was back.

My only regret about that night is that Lloydy wasn't there to see me play. A month earlier, I'd received the devastating news that he'd been found dead in his home after falling down the stairs. Even now, I'm still coming to terms with his loss. We weren't related but he was family and the only real father figure I've had in my life. He'd looked after me since I was 18 and we had a relationship that was so much more than player and agent. His lust for life was infectious and he seemed to be everyone's best mate. If you had a problem he would be the first to try and help you out.

He was the man about town in Manchester. Ryan Giggs released a statement revealing his shock and recalling their childhood together on the terraces at Old Trafford. He was also popular with the cast of *Coronation Street* after creating a celebrity football team who played in charity matches to raise money for various causes. It felt like half of the city was at his funeral; the street outside was flooded with people paying their respects. It was the perfect funeral, if there is such a thing, but it was heartbreaking to see his wife and daughter crying and saying their goodbyes. It was fitting that they played the Frank Sinatra song 'I did it my way' as he left the church. He really was a one-in-a-billion guy and I'm just thankful that he was part of my life.

Football was a coping mechanism in the months that followed. I knew there would be a comedown from my comeback and the following week I tweaked my back in training. It's pretty standard for players to suffer little niggles and knocks when they return from serious injury, so it wasn't a complete surprise, but it didn't go down well with Keith. 'Is that it then? Is that your season finished with? Do you even want to play football?' he said. As I walked off the pitch I took my gloves off and threw them in his direction. 'Give me a fucking break,' I said under my breath. After I'd calmed down, I explained to him that it was best for me to rest it for a week rather than trying to play through the pain barrier and risk a serious injury which could keep me out for months and undo all my hard work.

I could tell he wasn't happy, but I understood the pressure he was under. We'd played some brilliant football but found ourselves in the relegation zone after a bad run of form and a series of weather-inflicted postponements. He needed all of his players available for selection and to turn things around fast. Strangely, our fortunes fared better in the FA Cup. After beating Millwall in a fourth-round replay, we were drawn at home against Tottenham at the end of February. The game was on TV, meaning the club would get a big financial windfall, which was a big boost to our short-term future if we were relegated.

I'd been an unused substitute in both games against Millwall and was just happy to be named in the squad against Spurs. I was lapping up the pre-match atmosphere and preparing for our warm-up when our kitman, Jack, called me over and said Mauricio Pochettino wanted to speak to me. We always have a laugh and I thought he was pulling my leg but the ball boys said he was waiting for me in the tunnel. I wandered inside, half expecting to find I'd been the victim of a prank. 'Thompson, Thompson,' said Pochettino as I walked towards him. I'd learnt from my meeting with Pep and on this occasion I managed to keep my composure. 'How are you feeling? I've read about your story, it's incredible that you're back,' he said. We had a really good chat and he told me how much he loved the grittiness of lower league English grounds and how embedded the clubs were in the local community.

It was a touch of class and I understood after speaking to him and Guardiola why they've been so successful. They care about individuals and want to know the human as much as the player, which means they get the best out of them. A manager can have the best tactical brain on the planet, but if he lacks the personal skills to speak to players and understand their mindsets then he'll quickly lose the dressing room when they go through a bad run of form. The two Keiths, Hill and Curle, are the best managers I've worked under because they took the time to speak to me one-on-one and find out what makes me tick.

Keith needed all of his man-management skills to pay off if we were going to have a hope of beating Spurs. We had a few injuries, which meant some of the younger lads were given a chance. They didn't show any fear. Andy Cannon played out of his skin and wasn't unnerved at all by the occasion. He'd been immature when he'd been criticised in the past, but on the pitch his temperament was excellent and he grabbed the game by the scruff of the neck. We took the lead through Ian Henderson's goal just before half-time, but Lucas Moura and

Harry Kane scored in the second half and turned the game on its head. With a couple of minutes remaining of injury time it looked like we were heading out of the cup, but Steven Davies equalised with a brilliant finish to clinch a replay. He's struggled with injuries in recent years but he's the best finisher I've played with and you can tell he's played at a higher level. Me, Keith and everyone on the bench went mental and it felt like the stadium was shaking as the supporters jumped up and down. We were heading to Wembley.

Ten years had passed since I'd last visited Wembley and I didn't have happy memories of the place. I was left out of the squad for the League Two play-off final against Stockport and had to watch on from the stands as we were beaten 3-2. Keith brought it up in his pre-match team talk but reminded us all that whatever happened against Spurs we had good reason to celebrate after the game. The match was basically a free hit for us because nobody expected little Rochdale to cause an upset. I was on the bench again, but Chantelle, her sister Ruby, Lula and Reuben came to watch the game in the hope I'd come on and make a dream appearance. To run on at Wembley would be the perfect reward after the months of graft that I'd put in, but I also knew Keith couldn't and wouldn't just bring me on for emotional reasons.

It was -7°C in London and so much snow had fallen it was a surprise the game was still on. We went one-nil down when Son Heung-min scored an early goal, but Stephen Humphrys scored just before half-time to give them a fright. At the break, Keith told us to attack them and go for the kill, but in the end we ran out of gas and they picked us apart.

Perhaps we should've sat back and tried to nick a goal late on, but it's easy to say that in hindsight. Fernando Llorente scored a 12-minute hat-trick and Son bagged another to make it 5-1. It was game over and so Keith told me to go and warm up. With 64 minutes on the clock I ran on to the pitch with snow falling over Wembley. The stadium looked that big I felt like a gladiator entering an arena.

Keith had told me to play central midfield, which wasn't ideal given that I still wasn't fully fit. I knew I was going to have to use every ounce of my experience to get on the ball and cling to the coat-tails of some of their players. From the touchline the pace of Son and Moura had looked frightening. That's the biggest difference between Premier League players and those in the Football League. All of them were incredibly sharp and could change direction in an instant. They were perfectly honed machines with technical ability to match.

My job was made even harder when I injured my shoulder in a collision with Danny Rose. I stretched my arm out as I fell to the ground and heard a crunching sound. I immediately knew it was fucked. I couldn't raise my arm to hit long passes and crosses but there was no chance I was coming off. I didn't want the commentators on TV to be saying, 'Poor Joe Thompson, he's had such a tough year and now his big night has been ruined.' I'd had enough of being a sympathy case, so I just played through the pain barrier.

The game ended 6-1, but we'd done the club proud and headed back to Rochdale with our heads held high. After the game the physio had a look at me and told me I'd be out for a few weeks but thankfully I'd be fit enough to play a part in our run-in. He put my arm in a sling but I took it off and hid it in my bag when I did my interviews with the media after the game. I couldn't show any weakness. I was already the player who had survived cancer twice and I didn't want to be lumbered with a reputation for being weak and injury-prone. Once you've been given a label in football it's very difficult to shake it off.

On the journey home, I reflected on the last eight months. I was proud of myself, but didn't realise the impact of my story until I went on Twitter and saw my name trending in numerous countries. It was surreal seeing people on the other side of the planet tweeting about me. I wondered if my career would get any better than that night at Wembley. My contract was up at the end of the season and if we were relegated I'd either be released or offered reduced terms. If I left, what were the chances of me getting another contract with a Football League club? Playing under the arch at Wembley was incredible, but I still had more to give. Something told me there was one more chapter yet to be written.

Chapter 18

This Is Me

FOOTBALLERS and booze don't always mix well, but there we were, less than a week before the biggest day of the season, sinking pints in Manchester city centre on a Sunday afternoon like a group of giddy teenagers with fake IDs. It wasn't a quiet couple of pints, either; it was an all-day session with no curfew. Even better, we had the following day off to get our hangovers out of our systems.

Albert's Schloss Bavarian bar was the meeting point. Kick-off was 1pm. Late arrivals would be fined £50 and if you didn't turn up at all, the punishment was a hefty £200 fine. Guilty offenders wouldn't just have the lads to answer to, because it wasn't even our idea, it was Keith's. Unsurprisingly, everyone was prompt and our tables were soon full of steins of German beer and raucous laughter.

We had nothing to celebrate. We were in the relegation zone, two points adrift of safety ahead of the final game of the season, but the gaffer had decided the best way to galvanise the squad was for us to let our hair down away from the training ground. He also wanted us to get any issues off our chest over a few beers so any simmering tension would be relieved and wouldn't boil over during our relegation decider.

We didn't deserve to be in that position but that's probably what every team says when they're in the thick of a dogfight. Three weeks earlier, we'd blown a golden chance to pull away from the bottom three in a relegation six-pointer against local rivals Oldham. They had a spate of injuries in defence and were there for the taking, but Joe Rafferty had a second-half penalty saved after I'd been bundled over inside the box. We dominated the rest of the game but lacked the cutting edge to find the goal we needed and the game ended 0-0.

A draw was no use to us and afterwards I regretted not being firm and demanding that I took the spot kick. Don't get me wrong, Joe is a brilliant penalty taker and it was the first time I'd seen him miss one, but I was convinced it was written in the stars for me to score. I would've put the ball down and just put my laces through it, but by the time I'd got to my feet he'd already placed it on the spot. I went up to him and asked him if he was sure he wanted it and he was confident, so I left him to it. That's football, though, and we still had four games to try and beat the drop.

Bradford were up next at home but once again we threw away the chance to win three valuable points. We took the lead through Matt Done's first-half strike but in injury time my old mate from my Carlisle days, Charlie Wyke, popped up to equalise. It was another nail in our coffin and as I looked around the dressing room after the game, I started to wonder if it just wasn't meant to be. It felt like everything was going against us and mentally we were starting to crumble.

Keith had dropped me for that match, completely out of the blue, and I was worried if I'd feature in our remaining games. I'd been a bit late getting to the ground after being delayed by traffic, which meant my usual 30-minute journey to the stadium took two hours. When I walked down the tunnel, Beechy told me I wasn't in the squad without giving me an explanation. I thought it was a punishment but to my relief it turned out Keith was saving me so I was fresh for our final two games. We managed to grind out another 1-1 draw against a Plymouth team fighting for a play-off place, which did a little to restore our flagging morale, but we desperately needed a win.

An away trip to Oxford followed on the penultimate weekend of the season and once again the football gods conspired against us. Keith asked me to play right wing-back, but it's always a position I've struggled with. I'm used to operating 10 or 15 yards further up the pitch in a 4-3-3 or a 4-4-2, so I always find my distances aren't quite right. I often overcompensate defensively and end up about 15 yards too deep, and that was exactly what happened again. At half-time the opposition winger hadn't troubled me but I hadn't done anything to cause them concern in the final third and I was brought off before the hour mark.

Five minutes later we took the lead through Bradden Inman and briefly it looked like we were going to pull off a vital win and start our great escape. Unfortunately, that glimmer of hope lasted all of three minutes when Callum

Camps brought down his man and John Mousinho converted the penalty. Worse was to follow. With seven minutes of normal time remaining, Campsy conceded a carbon copy of his earlier penalty and Todd Kane fired home from 12 yards. The result moved Oxford eight points clear of the bottom three and secured their League One status, but we were now a point adrift of Oldham with just one game to go.

After the game, the dressing room was like a morgue. All you could hear was the sound of boot studs scraping against the floor and the Velcro shinpad straps being removed and tossed aside. I think a few of the lads thought we were down. I really felt for Campsy, who is a top young player, but he'll learn a lot from that afternoon. Like all good managers, Keith could sense the mood of the group and decided there was only one thing for it. 'I want you all out in Manchester tomorrow, every single one of you,' he said. A few of the lads exchanged glances. We thought he'd lost the plot. We asked him why, when we were all knackered and had a massive week ahead of us. 'I don't care what plans you've got tomorrow or what your missus is doing, pick a bar and meet there at 1pm.'

I rang my other gaffer, Chantelle, and told her I had no choice but to go out on a day session on Sunday. She was as baffled as I was but there was no getting out of it; she knows what Keith is like and thought better of trying to stand in my way. I joined the rest of the boys at 1pm sharp, but I wasn't drinking after deciding to knock it on the head after beating cancer. I've never been a big drinker, anyway, and can have a great time without getting off my face. There's no boozing culture in football anymore, like there was in the 80s and 90s, but I know players who like to have a few at the weekend and let their hair down. It's not for me, but if it's in moderation and it doesn't impact your recovery between games, then I think you can get away with having the odd beer.

The lads were a few pints deep when the insults started to fly. Campsy had to weather a few verbal blows about the two spot kicks he gave away. 'Don't trip him up mate,' said one of the lads when someone walked past him. Our centre-back Harrison McGahey also took a hammering from Keith. Harrison is a good young defender and the gaffer loves him, but he gets it in the neck every single day in training because he used to play in the same position and knows how much potential he's got. Harrison was like a young bull and tried to give a bit back but it was water off a duck's back for Keith. 'I don't care what you say, I'm going to keep hammering you on Tuesday and Wednesday and the day after until the penny drops,' he said.

It was 2am by the time I rolled into bed. It was a cracking night and when we all arrived at training on Tuesday morning, there was a real buzz around the place. Keith's plan had worked a treat. Somehow he'd turned an unhappy dressing room into a united one, ready for a final push for survival. We weren't going down without a fight. The gaffer decided to reveal his squad for the game several days early, so we could all prepare mentally. I was gutted to find out I was on the bench. There's nothing more frustrating than watching on and not being able to make an impact. I consoled myself with the thought that I still shouldn't have been anywhere near a football pitch, just being involved was a success in itself.

Our final day fixture pitted us against Charlton, who were flying high in the play-off places, while Oldham were away at Northampton, who had already been relegated. On paper the odds were stacked against us but Sky still picked us as their live game. In a way it felt like we were being set up for failure. In my head, I could already see the images of us trudging off the pitch after a gallant but unsuccessful attempt at a great escape. We were determined to avoid it at all costs and had three of the best days of training we'd had that whole season. Keith told the lads who weren't involved to train in a separate group and it helped to keep everyone focused. We couldn't risk any negativity spilling over and affecting morale.

I stuck to my usual routine in the build-up to the game. I don't believe in changing things just because the stakes are higher. You need to be focused, but also relaxed, and routine helps to create that mindset. On Thursday, two days before the game, I picked Lula up from her gymnastics class. She loves singing along to music in the car and on that particular journey she was belting out the soundtrack from *The Greatest Showman* at the top of her voice. I'm not going to lie, it isn't my sort of music, but on this occasion, there was a song, 'This Is Me', which caught my attention. It's a rousing track about refusing to give up, celebrating your scars and bruises, and triumphing through adversity. I added it to my pre-match playlist in the hope it might provide a bit of inspiration in the hours leading up to the game.

We were certainly going to need a showman or two if we were going to have any chance of pulling off a miracle. We were on TV, but I had no concerns that we'd suffer from stage fright, because we'd produced the best performance of our season against Tottenham in front of the BBC cameras. Some Football League players shrink when they're on Sky but our lads are never scared. Instead, they use it as an opportunity to show how good they are. I know I enjoy being in the spotlight because that's what you dream of when you're a kid, but there is an added pressure. You can play ten good games and then make one mistake on TV and people will make a split-second judgement about your ability. Even worse, your mates will give you stick about it for weeks.

I woke up early on Saturday morning to a sweltering hot day, as it always is on the last game of the season. Chantelle was flying to Dubai for a hair and beauty exhibition, so I had to get Lula dressed into her Rochdale shirt and then take her to my mum's house before they both headed to the game together. Chantelle was gutted to miss it. Normally she's in the stands for all my big matches, but she'd at least be able to watch it in the departure lounge at the airport.

It was a 5:30pm kick-off, so I got to the ground a couple of hours beforehand to start my preparations. The tunnel was busier than normal, with the TV crew setting up their equipment. There was a cameraman waiting outside the dressing room as I entered, which was a little reminder that we were under the microscope. I could feel the extra scrutiny when we were doing our pre-match warm-up, but I'm not one to get too serious and start playing up to it because it's just a drain on your reserves of energy. If I started posing and shouting at people to gee them up I don't think it would come across as authentic anyway and the lads would soon call me out for it.

Charlton are a very good side, but they made several changes, which gave us a lift. One of my mates from my Manchester United days, Nicky Ajose, had been rested, along with their big striker, Josh McGuinness, which meant they didn't carry their usual goal threat. They were in sixth place, three points ahead of Plymouth, meaning there would need to be a seven-goal swing to deny them a play-off place. Keith went for a 3-4-1-2 formation, which meant that if I entered the fray at any point, I'd probably come on in a wing-back or central midfield position.

Ten months of football had boiled down to 90 minutes. Over 5,000 fans had turned out, which was considerably more than we'd attracted for most of our home games, and a great turnout considering where we were in the table. I could sense the anxiety in the stands; everyone knew we'd face an uncertain future if we dropped into League Two. The referee blew his whistle, and the game started like a boxing match, with both sides throwing a few jabs, feeling each other out, and conserving energy in the heat.

I kept glancing up to my mum in the stands to try and find out the Oldham score. News filtered through that they'd gone 1-0 up early on, which would send us down. We couldn't allow ourselves to be distracted by what was going on in that game, though, we had to run our own race. Just before the break, Ian Henderson struck the post from close range as we edged the opening 45 minutes. It was a big chance, but we were boosted by the news Northampton had scored twice in a matter of minutes. If the scoreline stayed the same and we could find a winner, we would survive.

At the break, Keith told me and Steve Davies to warm up on the pitch. He wanted us primed and ready to come on at a moment's notice if he decided he needed more ammunition. We started the second half on the front foot and another ex-United team-mate of mine, Ben Amos, pulled off a brilliant save to deny Ryan Delaney's header. Charlton had a couple of efforts from distance but we were in control and just needed to find the cutting edge in the final third that we'd been missing for most of the season. With 67 minutes gone, Keith gave me and Steve the signal to get changed. My heart rate quickened a little bit. I was buzzing to get the chance to make an impact. There was a roar as we ran on to the pitch. Oldham had equalised, so we needed a goal or else we were down.

The crowd cheered every ball that went into the box and appealed even the slightest hint of a foul in the hope of getting a penalty. Two minutes after I came on, Joe Rafferty launched another cross into the box. Their centre-back headed it clear, sending Hendo crashing to the floor. Our fans went mental but the referee was having none of it, and Calvin Andrew headed the loose ball into my path. I had a quick scan around me and knew if my first touch was good, I could get a shot off on goal. As the ball came down, I shifted it from my right foot, on to my left. There was a sea of bodies in front of me, but there was just enough room for me to have a crack at goal. I got my head down and hit it as low and hard as possible with my left foot, towards the bottom right-hand corner.

There was a brief silence and then the net bulged. The stadium erupted. What happened next is a blur. I sprinted towards the corner flag to celebrate and chaos ensued all around me. Fans charged down the stairs and the whole squad ran over to join in the mayhem. My instinct was to rip my shirt off and jump into the stands but I knew I might get booked, which was the last thing I wanted with 20 minutes left.

In my head, a highlights reel of the last 12 months started to play. The bag of bones hooked up to a chemotherapy machine. The shivering wreck in the corner of the isolation room. The hours spent bent over a bowl being sick. The pain of my first run on the treadmill, which had nearly reduced me to tears. Training in the rain on my own with Kev and wondering if I'd ever make it back. This was the moment I'd been waiting for. This was me.

The game restarted and Keith barked instructions from the touchline. There were still 20 minutes remaining, but I was convinced we were staying up. It was fate. I wasn't nervous anymore, they could throw whatever they wanted at us but the script was written. In the stands, I could see everyone checking their phones. Charlton started to pump the ball into the box but we weathered a late storm and the final whistle blew. Full-time: Rochdale 1-0 Charlton. Fans started running on to the pitch, but we told them to calm down and wait, because the Oldham game still hadn't finished, which meant we faced an agonising seven-minute wait.

We didn't know what to do with ourselves. I grabbed Lula and put her on my shoulders so she could share the moment with me. Sky grabbed me and gave me their Man of the Match award, but my mouth was dry and I could barely string a sentence together. I headed into the tunnel and watched the final minutes of the game on a screen with a few of the lads. Keith sat in his office in complete darkness with his eyes closed. The seconds ticked by before the final whistle blew at last. Final score: Northampton 2-2 Oldham. We were staying up!

I ran to the dressing room and stuffed my shirt in my bag so I could get it framed, before joining the rest of the lads in the centre circle. Five thousand fans ran on to the pitch to celebrate and chanted, 'We are staying up, say we are staying up!' There were flares going off and all the supporters wanted to take selfies. In my head, I pressed pause for a minute and had a look around to take it all in. If you don't stop and take a mental picture then your memories can become a bit distorted. The moment was lost on Lula – all she wanted was to have a kickabout on the pitch with her two friends, Sebastian and Rachel, and found it all a bit weird that thousands of people were chanting daddy's name. She had to be patient; the party wasn't going to end any time soon.

I wouldn't normally celebrate surviving relegation, but this was different. The drama of the occasion and my goal was incredible. It was the best feeling I've ever had on a football pitch. It wasn't the best goal I've ever scored, but it was definitely the most important. I'm an ok finisher, but it's something I work on a lot with our coach, Tony Ellis. He's a born and bred Manchester man and was a prolific striker for Preston, Blackpool and a host of other clubs in the early 1990s. In training, he always wears his favourite pair of black Copa Mundials and his shooting is still lethal. Our finishing sessions are always at the end of training so we can practise under fatigue, and his advice is always the same, 'Low and hard, Joe, keep it low and hard.' If I hit the ball even six inches off the floor he'll pull me up for it.

After the chaos had calmed down a bit, I walked down the tunnel, and Tony was stood there. 'What did I tell you, Joe? Low and hard, keep it low and hard,' he said. We both burst out laughing. I'm just glad he didn't give up on me because all that practice paid off in the end. Stood nearby was Ben Amos, who congratulated me. It was surreal that I'd scored past him, having played in the same team as him for so many years at United. Football has a funny habit of throwing up these crazy moments of coincidence.

My overwhelming emotion was contentment. I owed the club big time for standing by me and paying my wages while I was ill and my team-mates for their constant support. That goal was a big chunk of my repayment to everyone from the chairman to our kitman, Jack. As I've said before, Keith isn't one to give me much praise, and he didn't say anything to me one-on-one after the game, but he did a few interviews saying how happy he was for me and that I deserved that moment after everything I'd been through. He knows how important my goal was for the club. Financially it was a lifesaver and, although I'm pretty sure he wouldn't have been sacked had we gone down, it could have saved his job.

A couple of hours later, I dropped mum and Lula off at home. She wanted to sleep with my Sky Man of the Match trophy, which is something I always did with my cross country and football medals as a kid. I was so happy she was proud of her dad.

The celebrations continued long into the night. People were queuing up to buy me a drink but I stuck to pineapple juice. The lads couldn't believe I wasn't having a few beers but there was no chance I was touching a drop.

It was the early hours of the morning by the time I got home. I checked my phone for the first time and was swamped with WhatsApp and Twitter messages. It was amazing to see how my story had transcended football. There were strangers suffering from all sorts of illnesses telling me how my story had inspired them. I watched the goal back on my phone in bed and couldn't believe how fast everything had happened. There were so many thoughts going through my head as I brought the ball down and fired it into the bottom corner, but you wouldn't know it. It was a very technical goal that I wouldn't have been able to score a few months earlier because it took so long for me to get my touch back. It was only at the end of the season that everything felt fluid and automatic again, which meant I could produce that touch and finish.

In the days that followed, I did countless interviews and was stunned that my story was even covered in America. I'd had a lot of media attention both times I'd been diagnosed with cancer, so it was nice to talk about what I'd done on the pitch for once. I also had a chat over the phone with my psychologist, Martin Robin Hall. He recalled my premonition when I was 22. My vision was that I'd score a winning goal in a blue kit and white Nike Vapors then carry a little boy on my shoulders after the game. Although it was a little girl sat on me and I was wearing a black pair of the same boots, it was scarily close to the reality of that final day. 'Believe in something and hold on to it,' he said. 'It might not have happened on the biggest stage, but you did what you always thought you would do.'

He was right; I had achieved my dream. It wasn't a title-winning goal for Manchester United at Old Trafford, in front of 80,000 people, but I'd saved my club in front of my people. Some top players go their whole careers without ever experiencing a moment like that. I realised this was how it was meant to be all along. My tough childhood in Bath, the pain of being released by United, surviving cancer twice; all of that adversity had given me the resilience to never give up. Had I not been through those setbacks, I may never have made my comeback and been stood on the edge of the box to score that winning goal. My football story had its fairytale ending but before I rode off into the sunset I needed to pay someone a visit.

Chapter 19
The visit

THE prison loomed large on the horizon, like a single dark cloud on a bright summer's day. It was surrounded by barbed wire fences and high walls as grey as a winter sky. Inside, hundreds of men were serving time for committing some appalling crimes. Among them was my father, who had been banged up for three years after being caught selling Class A drugs to an undercover police officer. It's a crime he still denies.

Nearly two months had passed since the final day of the season. After a three-week break in Miami with my closest friends and family, I'd spent the past few days in more humble surroundings, at a Haven caravan park in Weymouth, a short drive away from Dorset's Portland prison, building sandcastles and making memories with Lula and Chantelle. It was the sort of quality time I never spent with my dad and that was why I'd come to see him. I wanted answers to the questions that had haunted me since my childhood so I could let go of the past and move on with my life. I drove up a winding, narrow road, which I hoped would lead me to the truth. I pulled up in the car park and took a few deep breaths. For a moment, I considered turning around. 'Why should I miss an afternoon with my two girls for him?' I thought. I reminded myself that I wasn't doing this for dad, I was doing it for my own sanity. I was wearing a bright orange t-shirt like an American convict and was immediately greeted with suspicious looks from the prison guards as I stepped out of the car. I was raging inside. I felt like I was being judged for having connections to a prisoner. They didn't know anything about me but sadly their environment had taught them to trust no one.

I stepped inside the visitors' centre and was alarmed at the number of women waiting to see their husbands, boyfriends, sons and relatives. It showed the beauty of the female spirit. They were willing to stand by the men in their lives, despite the terrible things some of them must have done. My dad's girlfriend, Sarah, shares those same qualities. She's been in an on-off relationship with him for the past 15 years and I'd organised my visit through her son and my half-brother, Malachi. I'd been granted a two-hour slot, but I doubted if that would be long enough to talk over everything from the past 29 years.

Before I could see him, I had to show my passport to prove my identity and allow a sniffer dog to check me up and down, before a guard put a torch in my mouth to check I wasn't carrying drugs. One in five prisoners at Portland had developed addiction problems behind bars, which had prompted a rise in violence between inmates. The psychoactive drug spice had been smuggled in by visitors and was traded between lags, at a price even cheaper than tobacco. I was sure dad knew how to handle himself, but I deliberately left my ring and watch in a locker so his inmates didn't think I was a rich footballer and attempt to extort money from him for drugs.

I walked up a set of stairs, where a female guard was sat at a desk in front of a glass door. 'You must be Nicholas's son,' she said. 'He's been waiting a long time to see you, I can tell by the smile on his face.' She then asked me if I had any money I wanted to give him. 'Why would I give him money?' I said. 'He hasn't given me anything for years.' She rolled her eyes and laughed. 'He's over in the far corner.' I looked through the glass and saw him. He looked like a caged animal. He'd clearly been lifting a lot of weights to pass the time and was a lot bigger than the last time I'd seen him, when he visited me briefly with my auntie Jocklin shortly after I'd left hospital following my first battle with cancer.

The guard opened the door and I headed towards him, past four or five prisoners who were chatting to their loved ones. They all looked at me, nodded and gave me the thumbs up. Dad was clearly respected by his fellow inmates and must've had a reputation within the prison system. I wasn't impressed and wondered exactly what he'd done to earn his high rank. I suspected that fear was his weapon of choice, just like it'd been with my mum when I was a kid. He stood up and gave me a hug. 'I thought you wouldn't turn up,' he said. 'Good things come to those who wait,' I replied sarcastically.

We sat down and he pointed at a man two desks to my left who looked to be a similar age to me. 'That's your cousin, Josh,' he said. I was shocked. I knew I had other relatives behind bars but I'd never met him before. It was bizarre to think I had two family members locked up in the same prison wing on the south coast. Dad told me he was proud of me for everything I'd achieved and had watched me on TV in the FA Cup against Tottenham and on the final day of the season. He kept asking me questions, which was his way of using his charm to distract me from focusing on him and the real purpose of my visit. 'You know why I'm here, don't you?' I asked him. He nodded. 'You can ask me anything and I'll give you the truth,' he said. I wanted to believe him but he's a compulsive liar, capable of convincing himself of his own, made-up version of events.

I started by asking him why and how he'd ended up behind bars again. 'Plain and simple, I'm a mug, Joe,' he said. He was adamant that he'd been stitched up and hadn't sold drugs to an undercover officer. He even claimed he'd rumbled the policeman who was posing as a junkie after noticing he'd had a shave the day after first meeting him. 'I know who all the junkies are in Bath,' he said. 'Why would I be so stupid?' I found it hard to believe. He must've done something to get a three-year sentence, and even if he hadn't it was probably karma for all the misery he'd caused to other people over the years. I wanted to know if he was doing anything to change his ways. He said he was working as a painting and decorating instructor at the prison during the day, teaching younger inmates the tricks of the trade. It took me back to my mum's story about how they had first met, when he was painting the walls of the Women's Aid shop where she worked all those years ago.

I asked him to take me back to a time before I was born, so I could understand why his life had taken such a murky path. He explained that he'd become involved in crime in an attempt to make ends meet after mum had fallen pregnant with me. His first job was a burglary on a house close to where he lived. He'd watched the place for a month, along with several associates, to work out when the best time was for them to strike and the most vulnerable areas of the property.

One night, they decided it was time to get their loot. He crept towards the house and blowtorched the lead off the outside of the window before shoving it through. As he set foot inside, a dog started barking and his accomplices ran off down the street. Dad wasn't perturbed. He grabbed the dog, which he said was the size of a shoe, and locked it in a bathroom before carrying out the burglary and running off with his goods. After that night, he realised he had the nerve to operate in the underworld. The houses he stole from got bigger and so did the value of his haul, which he sold on to various jewellers. He was hooked.

What he did was wrong, and I'd never try and condone it, but a small part of me empathised with his desperation to provide for his family and newborn son. He also blamed his lack of education, which meant he had little hope of acquiring a serious job that would pay the bills to keep us afloat. Still, that didn't explain why he was missing for so much of my childhood. He blamed much of it on his addiction to drugs. He'd grown up in a Jamaican family who had a liberal attitude towards cannabis. He started smoking it when he was a teenager and then dabbled with pills and cocaine in nightclubs, along with my uncle Andrew, who worked as a bouncer in Bath. From there, his habit turned into an addiction and he started smoking crack. I looked at him in disbelief and asked him why he'd been so stupid. 'It gave me a buzz and took me to a place I'd never been to before,' he said.

He knew he had a problem and sought help from a doctor. He was prescribed methadone but stopped taking it after realising he was becoming addicted to that as well. His only solution was to resume his volatile relationship with crack and at one point he was taking up to £500 worth of the stuff a day. He found himself staying awake for days on end, unable to come down from the high, and turned to a dealer for help. 'He told me to take two hits of heroin a day,' he said. 'It gave me balance.' It reduced his spending on crack to £60 a day but he was now reliant on two powerful drugs to get by. I don't know how he afforded it but it was clearly his way of escaping his responsibilities and the reality of a life he didn't want. Drugs scare me, but he didn't seem to have any fear and I'll never understand why that buzz was greater than the one he would've got from bringing up his kids.

We started talking about mum. He told me he still loved her and always will do, but said his reckless personality and her bipolar disorder meant their relationship was always likely to spiral out of control. Surprisingly, he blamed her family for failing to address her mental health problems when she was a child. My grandparents said she was a hyperactive kid who would whistle and sing all day long. When you look back at old photos of her, she is wide-eyed and alert, but back then the condition hadn't been classified and my grandparents wouldn't have had a clue she was different to any other excitable young child. Ultimately, she needed an anchor in her life and dad couldn't provide it. He asked me how Lula was and wanted to know why I'd never sent him any pictures of her or replied to his letters. 'You should be making your own memories with her,' I snapped. He held his hands up in the air. 'Fair enough,' he said.

I still had more questions I wanted answers to but a guard informed me that my two hours were up. Before I left he asked me why Reuben hadn't visited, but I assured him he would do in time because he had questions of his own to ask. I also said that, despite everything, I wanted him to be part of the family again once he was out of prison. But, there was one condition. 'If you fuck up and get involved in any more bullshit then that's it for good, I'll cut you off,' I said. 'I understand,' he said and hung his head in shame. I stood up to leave and he handed me some beads. 'Say a prayer for me every night,' he said. 'Life's not easy in here.' Maybe it was because the other prisoners had left, but it was the first time he'd shown weakness and admitted to the difficulties of life behind bars. There had been a death at the prison and violence between inmates was a regular occurrence. Dad would need every ounce of his charm to keep himself safe.

On my way out of the prison, I got chatting to a woman and her daughter. Her son was in there for the second time. She just couldn't understand why he'd broken the law again, when he knew the reality of life behind bars. She wondered if he'd found his place in the prison hierarchy and felt at home there alongside people of a similar nature. The outside world was scarier, trying to find a job with a criminal record and resume friendships and relationships with people who had moved on with their lives. It's a vicious circle and that, in a nutshell, is probably the reason why my dad has reoffended so often. Only time will tell if he'll do so again.

I started the car engine and set off back to the caravan park in the afternoon sun. The first song on my playlist was 'Proud' by Heather Small. Lula loves to sing along to it and the lyrics summed up my emotions. I was proud that I'd stared the past in the face and felt I understood my dad better, even though I disagreed with his choices. I was also proud of what I'd achieved and overcome. I haven't seen and done it all but I've experienced a lot in my 29 years, which means I can empathise and help other people going through hard times. I wish things had been easier, but I don't consider myself to be an unlucky person. I've been blessed with an amazing life and have done things and been to places I dreamt of as a child. I have a beautiful wife and daughter and have played football for a living; in many ways I've been incredibly lucky.

Over the summer, I considered retiring from football, to avoid putting my body under any more unnecessary stress, but my doctor has reassured me that my major organs are all in good working condition. With each day that passes, there is less chance of my cancer returning, and it no longer preys on my mind. The future is bright; I have a life to live and goals to pursue. Away from the pitch, I'd love to have another child and give Lula a brother or sister to look after. I also want to use my story to inspire others and plan to start by helping a friend to get back on his feet. After returning to the caravan and turning on the TV, a yellow news strap snaked its way across the screen. 'Wolves goalkeeper Carl Ikeme in complete remission'. I smiled, opened the door and walked towards the light.